CAMPUS LANDSCAPE
PLANNING
& DESIGN

Edited by Michael Herz
Translated by Chang Wenxin

DESIGN MEDIA PUBLISHING LIMITED

CONTENTS

PREFACE

Culture and Modern Campus Landscape

The book takes a look at a subject area of public life which will become more and more important in the future: education. The prospective development of our societies will in future primarily be determined by the quality of culture and education.

How do we as planners deal responsibly with such a task? Which basic attitude regarding the public space and which understanding of the human being appear in spatial concepts? Which interactions emerge between spatial structure and the learning contents? How much do spatial structures at learning sites of all kinds define the understanding between individuals and society?

Fully astonished, we currently observe a globalisation of education: the international orientation of universities and schools, discussions across national borders on different educational and learning concepts. This development is not new; however, new is the range of this development and its (commonplace) penetration depth within the public life sector. In so far, the range of projects shown in this book is only coherent: across continents the presented projects come from Asia, America and Europe.

The following projects mirror a cross-section of all facets of different educational institutions: universities, secondary schools, primary and vocational schools, as well as schools for handicapped people. All sites have one thing in common: these institutions opened up for new ideas and concepts. The times in which structure and learning contents were determined by self-centredness are over. Instead openness and curiousity for learning determine the self-image of new generations. This does not only happen on the level of learning contents, it is also mirrored in the built structures. Which site could represent this new self-image better than the campus – the spatial and creative centre of the presented educational institutions.

The campus serves as a place of exchange of different cultures, ideas and working practices. However, it also acts as a kind of magnifying glass, tranporting the self-confidence of the institutions via spatial structures.

The tasks which have to be fulfilled by the planning are diverse and complex: this includes questions of organising spatial structures and their flexibility with regard to changed educational needs and contents; they integrate the state of the art of technology and the needs of modern educational and research institutions; they show a temporary and responsible use of natural resources and give an overview on the use of traditional and modern materials. However, a major thread of planning philosophy is visible in all these tasks: facilitating the highest possible level in self-determined learning.

The book displays modern examples of generating architectural and landscape qualities of the site and their interactions. Today, the consequent integration of architectural and landscape architectural concepts to form a coherent whole determines the quality of planning for different needs and in different yardsticks. From the complete concept to the details, here the usability for future users and the adaptability to future developments, which we are not yet able to see, are manifested. For us planners, the creation of significant spatial structures and their interpretation ability still poses one of the largest challenges.

As already described at the beginning, we notice an opening of traditional educational institutions as universities and different school establishments. This not only happens on the level of the educational institutions themselves – they increasingly influence the development of complete cities and districts. With them opening up, educational institutions become a component in the city. They substantially influence the development of the surrounding area – as regards living, commerce, services and/or trade.

Within the network of the city's public spaces, the modern campus turns into an attractive address with effect. It not only incorporates the claim to a modern city and educational landscape, but also integrates different cultures and life designs.

With designing new campus landscapes educational establishments of all kinds receive a distinct profile. They are (apart from some other factors) important components of building an identity, which shines far beyond the institution: they become a catalyst of modern urban and landscape development in the 21st century.

Michael Herz
20th November 2012

Figure1 The new buildings, parking lot and outdoor activity spaces are integrated, which helps to establish a friendly relationship between the buildings and the environment as well as create leisure and communication spaces for students.
Figure2 The Perry School site was an empty expanse of pavement with parking extending through the schoolyard, a desert programmatically and environmentally. Through a consensus based community process with the school, neighbourhood, Boston Schoolyard Initiative and City of Boston, the landscape architect David Warner designed the Boston Harbour Island themed schoolyard and outdoor classroom richly detailed with maritime influences.
Figure3 Courses at outdoor classrooms

1

CHAPTER ONE: INTRODUCTION

1.1 Meaning and trend of campus landscape design

Campus planning and landscape design offer opportunity to realize transformational change, promote distinctive, welcoming and sustainable places in which to learn and live. External environments can form the focus of campus communities, providing spaces and places for social interaction, rest and relaxation, recreation, exchange of ideas and support a strong sense of ownership and belonging. (Figure 1)

Current trend in campus design emphasize is integrating school planners, local planning and zoning departments, transportation (vehicular and pedestrian), public works and parks departments in the planning process to create an integrated and cooperative process.

1.2 Characteristics

1.2.1 A high-quality schoolyard is multi-use and multi-task.
The campus is suitable for innovative learning and creative-play activities as well as traditional recreation. The site is also open to community and out-of school programmes allowing for highest use and offering benefits to the greatest number of people possible.

The site design and procedures are flexible and adaptable to changing and evolving usage.

1.2.2 A high-quality campus begins with an inclusive design process.
A high-quality campus facilitates and encourages developmentally appropriate play and learning activities through its design, which means that experts on principles of cognitive development and age-appropriate play work with architects in the design phase. (Figure 2)

Furthermore, the design phase also emphasizes community participation, allowing the broadest possible range of potential users to give input. Through this process, the design responds to local needs and creates a sense of local ownership of the campus.

1.2.3 A high-quality campus fosters partnership with community organizations.
Strong reciprocal relationships between schools and other community organizations form around high-quality campuses. By sharing the site, schools provide a valuable resource to community organizations and at the same time, schools benefit from the resources and expertise of partner organizations. A participatory planning stage can initiate the development of these partnerships even before the physical site exists, which enhances the utility and long-term sustainability of the campus.

1.2.4 A high-quality campus is integrated into the educational planning process.
High-quality campuses are an integrated part of the school's learning curriculum, and serve as the site for teaching of traditional disciplines as well as interdisciplinary activities.

The school [policy] environment enables the integration of indoor and outdoor activities by allowing teachers the flexibility of scheduling, planning and assessment they need to take an innovative approach to teaching in the campus. (Figure 3)

1.2.5 High-quality campus fosters continuity of use.
By encouraging broad participation in the planning and design process, by fostering high levels of use by a range of community organizations and by integrating learning activities into the curriculum, high-quality campus creates a 'culture of use' that ensures the continuity of activities and benefits from year to year.

1.2.6 High-quality campus demonstrate sustainability.
High-quality schoolyards engage in environmentally friendly practices to ensure the longevity of the built and the natural environment. Maintenance of the physical site is considered from the beginning, starting in the planning and design stage, and is treated as an ongoing process – not a one-time investment.

CHAPTER TWO: DESIGN CONCEPT

Well-designed campus helps conserve the environment and foster greater environmental awareness and stewardship. Well-designed campus creates a learning environment that stimulates improved teaching and learning. Well-designed campus reduces the likelihood of injuries and is the site of fewer incidents of crime and vandalism. When crime and vandalism decrease on and near campus, the value of the surrounding property increases. (Figure 4)

The ideal campus is designed to address three areas of activity:

2.1 Recreation and Physical Education

The development of motor skills, physical fitness, the ability to work & play together in groups, and enhanced self-esteem are a few benefits seen from the installation of play structures, physical challenge courses, and properly maintained fields and courts. (Figure 5)Many schools lack adequate gymnasium space and students will expend their energies in the hallways or classrooms if not given a more appropriate outlet. During out-of-school time, facilities should be open to neighbourhood youth and families, local sports leagues, and summer camps.

2.2 Social Development

Well-designed campus not only contribute to the physical development, but also to the psycho-social development of young children, by providing spaces where children can practice new developmentally appropriate behaviour and apply it to new situations, as evidenced by: performance and mastery of developmentally appropriate skills.

Part of learning and growing up involves the ability to function in a group setting. In the campus, whether formally or informally, youth have the opportunity to form

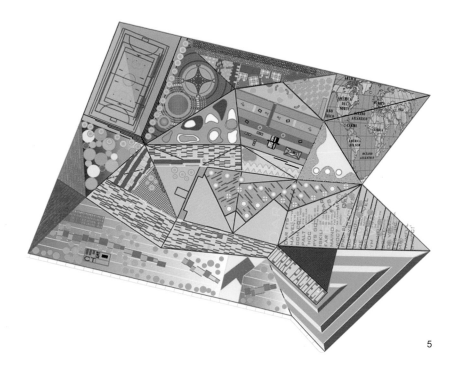

Figure4 The simple, orderly and practical landscape design brings the buildings and their surrounding together, forming a multi-use space for services, education and recreation
Figure5 Playing facilities and sports field

5

groups, reach consensus, and develop critical thinking and problem-solving skills with their peers. These interactive skills will aid students as they enter the 'real world' where the ability to cooperate with colleagues in the workplace may be more important than remembering the Pythagorean theorem. Although a sad commentary, it is true that many urban youth are not allowed outside their houses or apartments without close adult supervision. Working parents instruct their children to come home from school and lock the doors behind them. Supervised time in the campus may be the only opportunity children have to be outdoors. Expanded access through outdoor classes, after school programmes and summer camps will address this very basic human need. (Figure 6)

2.3 Academic Learning

Well-designed campuses are learning environments that contribute to improved academic learning, by providing a hands-on environment where children can gain learning skills and apply new knowledge and information.

Outdoor, experiential learning is a teaching methodology that can add a new dimension to public education. Any subject that can be taught inside a classroom can be taught as well, and perhaps better, outdoors. For example, many schools are experimenting with planting trees, working on gardens or nature areas. The act of planting and caring for a tree, observing its growth cycles throughout the year, and discussing its niche within the surrounding built or natural ecosystem, is a "learn by doing" activity that can be conducted in most campuses. Compare this with the more traditional practice of pouring through chapters of a text or the more recent practice of sitting before a computer or video monitor. Of course, indoor and outdoor classrooms can, and should, work to compliment each other. Abstract and theoretical notions can often be applied, or put to practical use, in the context of outdoor hands-on class projects. Campus/schoolyard learning activities also lend themselves to a multi-disciplinary approach. A school garden can be an instructional tool for teaching math (measuring & counting), science (environment), literacy

6

(journal writing), social studies (urban agriculture) and art (scarecrows). Many campus projects also lend themselves to community service learning by interacting with the surrounding neighbourhood.

As with the school building, the use of the campus/schoolyard is dependent upon the condition of the facility and upon the site's programmatic content. Traditionally, campus has been seen as recreational open spaces that may contain ball fields and courts or play structures. At worst, they may have become unsafe vacant lots or parking annexes. Over the past several years, we have seen an emerging effort to tie school grounds to the core mission of the school – teaching & learning. The concept of the outdoor classroom has captured the imagination of local education advocates and practitioners have been actively engaging students in a variety of hands-on, experiential learning activities. From mapping and measuring to gardening and meteorology, to drama productions and student-drawn murals, we are witnessing a pedagogical surge that combines the best aspects of creative play and academic learning. The campus of the 21st century is a multi-use site that fosters recreational, academic, and social activities and strives to weave its functionality into the fabric of school and community culture. (Figure 7)

Figure 6 The design for the James Square reflects current educational and social needs while respecting the historic heritage of McGill University's 19th century buildings. The design goal was to create a coherent space where social and academic life could comfortably and safely extend into the outdoors.
Figure 7 The Perry School is located in the dense residential City Point neighbourhood of South Boston with direct views to Dorchester Bay and the Boston Harbour Islands. The programme requirements for outdoor play are established to maximise opportunities for active and imaginative play. BSI's primary goal is to 'transform schoolyards into dynamic centres for recreation, learning and community life.'

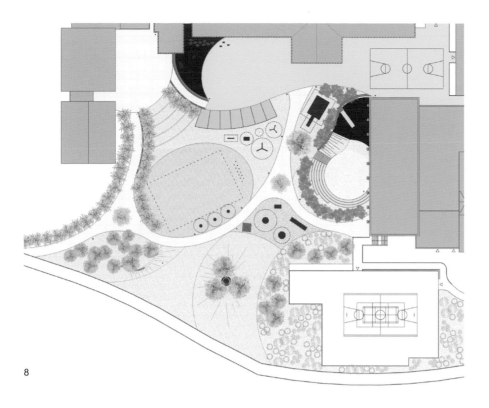

8

CHAPTER THREE: CATEGORIES AND CHARACTERISTICS

3.1 K–12

3.1.1 Primary School

The designers should make maximum use of the site provided which should be reflected in their design proposal. The layout should be designed to minimise the need to dispose of excavated material off-site.

The site constitutes the building, playing fields, any agreed supplementary area, and access which should be designed to ease the management of the school. Sites should generally be of regular shape, reasonably level, good road frontage, be without obstruction and have reasonable space for developing a set-down/pick-up area. (Figure 8)

Landscaping should be simple, cost effective and easy to maintain. The Designers should consider the natural paths and routes through the site to the school entrances in determining the appropriate location and the extent of paths provided. Large areas of hard landscaping should be avoided.

Design Teams should consider the design of landscaping elements to promote more imaginative play and complement the teaching environment in their design proposals. External space for planting, weather recording, sundials etc., should all be explored. Such shrubs and trees should help define the site boundaries and external circulation routes, and should be hardy, durable and low maintenance.

In new schools, the hard surfaced games courts and junior play area should be provided as specified in the schedule of accommodation. The area of hard play is inclusive of ball-courts and junior play but exclusive of roads, paths, etc.

In the case of an extension to an existing school, the existing hard courts should

be retained where possible. Laying out a variety of courts within a single multi-use games area makes supervision easier and extends the range of games. The location of the hard play area should be considered in the context of future expansion of the school in order to eliminate future disruption, nugatory expenditure, and rebuilding at a later stage.

Hard-play areas may be designed to cater for occasional use as overflow car parking and should be located adjacent to the external vehicular circulation. The location of play areas shall be integrated into the external environmental education plan. Separation of Junior and Senior hard play areas should be agreed in discussion between the school and the Department.

A ball-court area includes a run-off space around the playing area and shall be properly graded, drained and appropriately lined. Poles with hoops and backboards for basketball shall be supplied and fitted. The courts shall be marked for basketball and a high power coated weld mesh fence around the courts, with lockable access gates provided. Where more than one court is provided the fence should surround the group of courts and not individual courts. Sockets shall be provided at the half way point on each court for possible future installation of volleyball poles and net. (Figure 9)

Adequate surface water drainage shall be provided from all hard play areas without compromising the safety of user during play. In providing such drainage, consideration must be given to the possibility of some games being played across the basketball courts. A duct with draw wire should be provided to allow for possible future services to hard play areas from the nearest internal services position (e.g. plant room/switch room/store etc.).

The residual site area of the external play areas after the development of hard play area should be seeded for grass. Where site area and configuration permits, an area should be reserved suitable for use as a practice playing field.

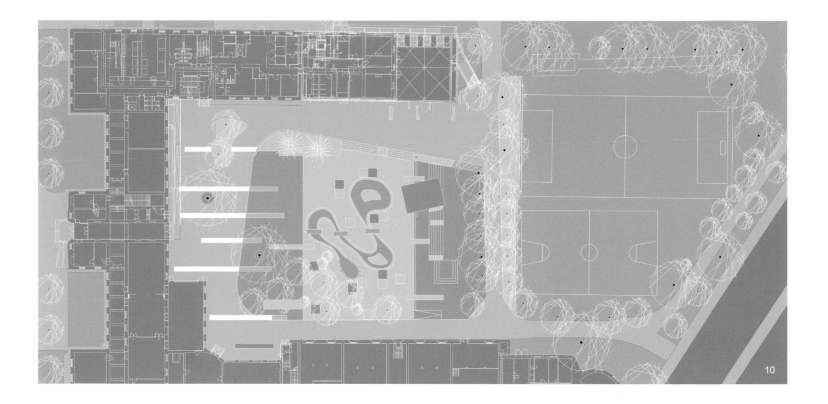

3.1.2 Middle/High School

Schoolyards and outdoor areas for middle and high school grade levels need a master plan of their own with special consideration to the relationship to the school building.

An education programme developed by the staff and administration for the site should identify the experiences and activities that will take place outside the school building. Basic principles for design of outdoor space should include discussions of the need for organized sports, social gathering space, natural areas for environmental education, community activities, and open space for exercise, running and physical education activities. (Figure10)

Access for the students from the school to the outdoors is important. Direct access from the locker room is the preferred arrangement. Additional parking space must be considered if spectators are anticipated for sports activities or after-school activities. An additional challenge must be the accessibility to all areas for students with disabilities. (Figure 11)

Figure9 Basketball field are fenced to protect the students.
Figure10 The master planning includes sports and activity spaces, outdoor educational spaces, gathering spaces, rain garden, etc.
Figure11 Existing roads have been reused to create a grid of paths, square and green belts which has connected all the facilities in the school. Walls and fences forms the boundary of the school.

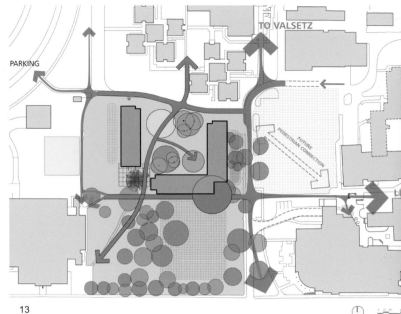

Additional design considerations should include:
• Barriers and perimeter outlines
• School property line boundary designation
• Stable, paved pathways to allow all students to reach outlying areas
• Lighting
• Adequate trash can placement
• Bicycle racks
• Storage areas for equipment
• Clear sight lines over entire schoolyard and field areas for supervision
• Signage indicating age-appropriate equipment
• Easy access for maintenance trucks and equipment

The design of athletic programmes presents a challenge for schools striving to accommodate increasing numbers of participants and activities. Lack of space for fields is especially problematic in urban areas.

Natural grass remains the standard for sports fields, but new developments in synthetic turf technologies have created multiple options where there is a shortage of land for fields. Grass is difficult and expensive to maintain properly because constant use is hard on high-traffic areas. Even though the initial expense is greater for artificial turf, the cost of upkeep can be significantly reduced.

Middle school age children present a particular problem. Their schedules should allow for some outdoor recreation time in addition to physical education. The space allowed should be larger than the area allotted to younger students and should be less constrained. Open space for pick-up games and running should be part of a design. These students are usually not involved in interscholastic sports so access to fields is more limited but structured competitive sports still require the availability of fields. An amphitheater is ideal for this age group. (Figure 12)

Outdoor time is important and some developmentally appropriate equipment

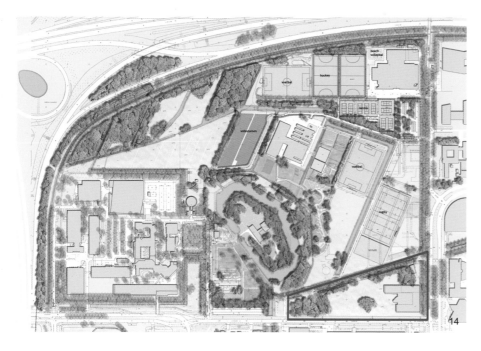

Figure12 Athletic facilities on the playground
Figure13 Master planning of Ackerman Hall in the Grove
Figure14 The master planning includes streets around the buildings, roads and paths, green belt, courtyard, square, garden and playground. The area marked in red is the renovated area.

should be provided during the school day or lunch time and could include:(Figure 12)
• Rope or chain climbers on angles
• Climbing apparatus
• Horizontal bars and ladders
• Sliding poles
• Balance beams
• Benches and chat areas that allow for gender separation
• Built-in chess boards
This age group should be included in schoolyard design discussions. Even if space is limited, middle school students have definite ideas about their needs for recreation and relaxation.

3.2 Higher Education

The purpose of a campus is to bring together diverse people and their ideas in an environment that creates potential for intellectual and social exchange. Both its buildings and its open space define the physical character and quality of a campus. The design intent for both building and landscape projects should include promoting a sense of community derived from actively shared spaces that provide enriching experiences of both planned and chance encounter. (Figure 13)

Campus spaces are developed to serve educational purposes (horticultural gardens or arboreta), entertainment purposes (playing fields, amphitheaters) and to enlighten users of the landscape by incorporating sculpture and other forms of art into the design. Campus landscape should be designed into a green environment that situates, serves, and symbolizes higher education. Comprised of exterior spaces (including streets, walkways, greens, courtyards, plazas, gardens and playing fields) and interior spaces (lobbies, atriums and internal connectors), community space has the potential to weave together the diverse elements for the campus and maximize the opportunities for intellectual and social exchange. (Figure 14)

Figure15 Private sitting area with planting screen
Figure16 Seating area with umbrellas
Figure17 Seats on the wall
Figure18 Steps for sitting
Figure19 Custom seating with lightings
Figure19 Activites

Design of campus landscape space has been overlooked for years. With many institutions expanding and renewing their campus, the importance of campus landscape space has gained its rightful due. The current trend in the design of public open space and the healthy active living both indicate the importance of the users' involvement in the design process. For university campus, it is easy to identify the majority end-users of campus landscape spaces are students. Faculty, staffs, parents, visitors and surrounding community members are also important users. How to bring users' voices into the design becomes an important task for design professionals.

For example, most college students' needs for campus garden include the followings:

- Sitting Places (Figure 15- Figure 19)
- Naturalness, trees & greenery
- Grass & open space
- Peace & quietness
- Feeling Free & comfortable
- Fresh Air
- Shade/Sun
- Safety
- Clear
- Activities(Figure 20):
  - Studying/Reading
  - Recreation
  - Socialing
  - Conversation
  - Eating
  - Family gathering
  - Meditation
  - People watching
  - Sun bath

Figure21 Grass and trees on the roadside help to create
a joyful walking experience.
Figure22 Seating and paths to the building entrances are provided.

Now, colleges and universities also emphasize the importance of active living on campus. Some colleges and universities redesign their campus adopting some active living principles, such as:

• Keeping the campus 'walkable' with comfortable pedestrian and open space corridors
• Vehicular traffic will be allowed to remain where needed, but only calm traffic on pavements that complement the pedestrian environment and scale
• Pedestrian corridors should have continuity of comfortable elements (Figure 21)
• Continuity of pavement types
• Concrete pavements with finish and texture that can be easily repaired and replicated. Special brick or other unit pavers should be used in limited special areas only. Concrete paving is more feasible and affordable to maintain and replace. Unit pavers in disrepair are unsightly and can be dangerous. Concrete pavement can be given more human scale and texture by using closely spaced saw joints and similar techniques
• More emphasis on comfortable, clean, safe usable grass open spaces (Figure 22)
• Comfortable benches and furniture for outdoor study and informal gatherings in shaded and protected locations
• Meeting areas in appropriate quiet settings
• Avoid unnecessary obstacles such as raised planters where direction or space definition is not provided
• Provide a tree lined green strip between sidewalk and curb, especially on campus edge streets

3.3 Special Education

In developing an approach to the design of facilities for pupils with special educational needs, it is important to have a shared understanding of what is meant by the term 'special educational needs' and what is endeavoured to be achieved in developing this particular approach. Pupils with special educational needs have

Figure23 The Chartwell School is a certified LEED Platinum private school for children with dyslexia. The campus is designed to facilitate the development of the frequently exceptional capabilities of dyslexic children by providing an emphasis on the arts and the woodland environment.
Figure24 Large 'Green Wall' for aurally handicapped people, creating a delightful educational environment

many characteristics in common with each other and with those who do not have special educational needs. It is however also acknowledged that pupils with special educational needs form a heterogeneous group with each pupil having distinctive individual and specific strengths and needs. (Figure 23)

There are two key objectives in meeting the challenges posed by providing for pupils with special educational needs. These are concerned with promoting the principles of
• Inclusivity: recognizing and accepting diversity; valuing each pupil as an individual
• Flexibility: ability to modify spaces to suit different user groups and ability to use spaces for different purposes

While the emphasis will be on providing a pleasant environment certain factors must be taken into account in the selection of materials and the detailing and design of services etc. to ensure the safety of all. (Figure 24) Some pupils may become quite distressed and occasionally exhibit challenging behaviour. The correct selection and appropriate detailing of materials, finishes and fittings should eliminate opportunities for self-injury. Above all, facilities must be sufficiently robust to cater for all eventualities.

Designers are advised to carry out a risk assessment of the general site conditions and landscaping around the school and plan for risk mitigation or elimination. A typical example would be a natural watercourse or stream flowing through or adjacent to the site, or a pond or open fire fighting reservoir. Such items might not pose specific risks for mainstream pupils but for pupils with special educational needs, and as such, may create unacceptable risks which should be designed out. External play should be provided in a secure location which is close to, and ideally directly accessible from, the classrooms for pupils with special educational needs.

CHAPTER FOUR: INTEGRATED DESIGN

4.1 Intent

Achieve an effective collaborative design process and outcome by engaging the multiple design disciplines, as well as users, constructors, facility managers and operations personnel.

4.2 Requirements

- Assemble a design team to peliorm integrated functions
- Team members must represent at least three of the following disciplines:
Architectural/residential design
Landscape design, civil engineering, habitat restoration, land planning
Green building/sustainable design
Mechanical or energy engineering
Building science or peliormance testing
- Actively involve members mentioned above in at least three of the following:
  Conceptual/schematic design
  LEED planning
  Preliminary design
  Energy/envelope design or analysis
  Design development
  Final design, working drawings or specifications
  Construction
- Conduct regular meetings with team members on project updates, challenges, solutions and the next steps (Figure 25)

4.3 Strategies

Use cross-discipline design and decision-making, starting early in the process and continuing throughout to take advantage of interrelationships between systems. Include representation early on in the design process from end-user stakeholders, including administration, facility planning staff, facility operation staff, faculty and students. Provide for feedback from all participants.

25

Figure26 Rochester Institute of Technology (RIT) Global Plaza

CHAPTER FIVE: PLANNING PROCESS AND DESIGN PROCESS

In campus planning, design professionals whose focus is the outdoors must be sensitive to transitions from building to open space, the need for common areas and the protection of special features. These design professionals must also be able to use plant and building materials and site furniture to enhance the use of the outdoors for study, relaxation, contemplation, socializing and entertainment. (Figure 26)

5.1 Recommendations

Achieving the goal of creating high performance campus requires a deliberate and inclusive planning process. The following recommendations are off ered with this goal in mind:

• A starting point for determining minimum site size includes calculating the sum of the building footprint, schoolyard, one or more playfields, secure parking, and green space

• Campus should include where possible a multipurpose area that may be used for field games and organized play. Such activities may include touch football, soccer, field hockey, softball, or little league baseball. Regulation sized fields for any of these activities, although desirable, are not necessary when land is just not available

• The planning process should be closely coordinated with the municipal master plan and with the staff of the local government

• The planning process should be designed with the active participation of all stakeholder groups – teachers, maintenance staff, community residents, municipal and district officials, youth groups, crime watch programmes and students

• Opportunities to participate in the design process should be provided to students at all grades to enrich the educational experience of students while improving the ultimate design of the project

Figure27 The Tulane University Centre project includes the redesign and expansion of the existing university centre and surrounding campus area. The landscape architect conducted extensive research on the best building practices to withstand constant fluxes in climate such as flooding, tropical storms, hurricane force winds, and extreme heat and humidity. Research on the climatic conditions and best construction practices for this region was critically important to the outcome of this project.

• An interdisciplinary team of professionals— educators, architects, landscape architects, engineers, municipal officials and others should guide, not dominate, the process

• The planning and design process should maximize the unique topographic, climatic and locational aspects of the site to create a schoolyard that is representative of the environmental, architectural and historic attributes of the area. (For example, a schoolyard developed on a brown fields site can incorporate a small area showing the prior underground brown fields condition – providing a unique learning opportunity.)In fact, a section of the campus or the entire yard may reflect an environmental, architectural or historical theme consistent with the context of the area (Figure 27)

• Opportunities for partnerships with community groups, Community Development Corporations, and private or public employers should be sought at the planning stage. These partnerships can provide capital assistance, as well as ongoing maintenance and programme support

• The planning process should be closely integrated with the pedagogical philosophy and goals of the district and school. The planning process should centre first on providing space for activities in physical education. It can then be extended to include science, language arts, social studies and math. Finally, the planning process should address the quality of life issues of the students, faculty and community

• Periodic public meetings of the stakeholder group should be scheduled at times and in locations conducive to public participation

• The final design shall include both an analysis of the maintenance requirements and costs of the area and the resources required to insure that adequate maintenance and operation of the area will occur

• The use of natural materials – water, dirt, vegetation, animals, wood – should be given first priority in design

• Larger sites should consider creation of meadows or other environmentally rich landscapes rather than simply planting grass over the site

• The campus should be a tool for learning itself – by incorporating physical features such as sundials, maps designed into the play surfaces, murals, and labeling of materials, flora and fauna

• The design process should consider leaving one or more areas of the campus 'undesigned' so that the users can assess the functioning of the campus and add – or remove– additional equipment or features. This may be able to occur through involving the community in the construction or reconstruction of the campus though a 'community build day'

All aspects of campus landscape development, from the first design impulses to the definitive programmatic statements, will benefit from an analysis of the site's visual character. Physically each campus is different in its wholeness and in detail. Concepts and proposals best begin with an appreciation of the significant existing physical circumstances and conditions that appear to give a site its perceptible distinctions and the relationships of those elements to one another, including the environs. Surveys may reveal complex or simple conditions, but not necessarily related to institutional size or acreage.

At existing campuses a customized account of the visual character will help illustrate and communicate the pluses and minuses of the existing campus landscape and thus set the agenda for improvement and extensions. As each campus is different, so is the descriptive vocabulary. The information can be displayed in map form, supplemented by photographs and narration. Typical coverage would include the campus edges, entrances, exits, boundaries, open spaces and their functional variations, architectural landmarks, specimen landscapes, circulation networks and the manner in which they give structure to the overall campus design, views and vistas, and a depiction of the good, the bland, and the ugly.

Occasionally visual character analysis will reveal opportunities for some early action, a landscape proposal that would self- evidently help remedy a deficiency that didn't require a total plan. Early actions can also help gain support for the process and product, being a kind of reward for participation in the planning process.

5.2 Case Study

CMG Landscape Architecture collaborated with Marin Country Day School and EHDD Architecture in 2006, to develop a 25-year plan for the existing K-8 private school and then subsequently designed phases 1 and 2 of the plan. The school's campus is nestled in a valley formed by the serpentine ridges of Ring Mountain. Historically, the valley was filled with meandering streams and tidal marshes that drained the 70-acre Ring Mountain watershed into the San Francisco Bay. Protecting and restoring this ecosystem, as well as providing opportunities for students to interact and learn from this habitat, has been driving the pedagogy and development of the school and its curriculum. CMG's work began with a study of broader ecological and human systems that formed the existing campus' landscape. CMG collaborated with the architects on the building massing and structure of the campus' open space, circulation, and natural system integration. A goal was to identify curriculum connections to the material fabric of the campus that included opportunities for native habitat restoration, educational hydrological relationships, and academic rituals.

Phase 2 includes a redesign of the entire east side of the campus: a new Learning Resource Centre, the Step Up Amphitheatre, a new Lower School Playground, Lower/Middle/Upper School Art Studios, Lower/Middle/Upper School Classroom renovations, and a Creek Restoration of the perennial stream that runs along the eastern length of the valley. (Figure 28)

The story of water's interaction with this valley encouraged the team to explore all water integration possibilities in the new design of phase 2: rainwater harvesting, greywater reuse, stormwater filtration, and native stream restoration. The new Learning Resource Centre collects all rainwater roof runoff and stores it in a 15,000 gallon underground cistern below the Lower School Playground; the water is then reused in the building's heating/cooling system and for flushing toilets. Water meters monitor and report the amount of rainwater collected from the rooftops and used for the greywater system — to create a comparison against the amount of potable city water usage. All project site stormwater is filtered through a system of natural cleaning devices integrated in multiple locations on the east side of campus. Upper school play area and classroom roof runoff water is directed to the upper school bioswale and filtered through native wetland plants before being released into the nearby creek. The bioswale is spanned by Bench/Bridges to highlight spatial awareness and create gathering spaces integral with the natural system. The Lower School stormwater is directed to a bioswale north of the Lower School Classrooms which is planted with 'fantasy play plants' — like Money Trees or Corkscrew Willows which have seed pods or interesting branches — that the children can use to create crafts and make-believe games. Finally, all treated stormwater flows into the restored creek and out to the Bay.

Figure 28 Overall view of phase II

29

Figure29 Part of a wider development for the facilities at Victoria University's Footscray Park Campus, RWA was engaged to re-develop two of the major courtyard spaces within the campus – the Eastern and Western Courtyards. Both courtyards needed to function at both campus level and courtyard level.
Figure30 The northern St Francis Courtyard focuses on a central water feature. This historical core was retained with new paving and planting to adjoining garden areas. Large sandstone rectangular rocks provide seating around a circular path and allow for a subtle transition between changing heights and slopes.
Figure31 Planting consisted of a mix of Australian, European, South African and Japanese plant species. The objective was to achieve year round interest, foliage throughout winter months and a rich floral display throughout spring and summer. Silver was used generously to compliment the contemporary building and surrounding Eucalyptus trees.

CHAPTER SIX: DESIGN ELEMENTS

6.1 Courtyards

Courtyards are typically defined as an open space with a building or walls on all four sides. Spaces surrounded on three sides by a building or walls with an open end can also be classified as courtyards.

Courtyards are often adjacent to building entries, to provide places for seating and public interaction. Courtyards in campus provide not only light for rooms within buildings, but can also provide restful scenery to alleviate eye fatigue and provide a distinctly different environment for learning.

The most successful courtyards are those that have a sense of enclosure, provide a variety of seating opportunities and have a high level of refinement in materials. (Figure 29)

Below is a list of elements to include as the groundwork for a successful courtyard:
• Analyze sun angles, building massing and orientation to ensure the most positive impact on the quality of light both into the courtyard and into the adjacent spaces
• Provide for south light or place the courtyard at south of the building as much as possible with appropriate shading
• Note the direction of prevailing winds and design for protection
• Consider the access needed by both personnel and equipment to provide regular maintenance. Snow removal should be taken into account
• Plant native species
• Before the trees mature, shade may be provided by arbours, pergolas, fabric structures, umbrellas, etc.
• Consider drainage patterns, porosity of the path material and its impact on storm water management. Provide good drainage, not only to collect the water, but also

discharge the water to a safe place
• Provide the appropriate surfaces for the intensity of foot traffic expected
• Create 'places' within the courtyard through material changes, elevation changes and landscaping (Figure 30)
• Design the courtyard and its surrounding uses so they can 'be good neighbors' to one another(Figure 31)
• The location of low walls can distinguish a picnic table area for eating and reading from a class gathering area where the low wall acts as seating. Grassy areas and sidewalks reinforce the different activities. Planting boxes and beds can border the entire perimeter of a courtyard
• Create a sense of layering from the enclosed building environment out to the fully exposed courtyard using arburs, pergolas, and architectural items such as semi-enclosed porches
• Courtyards and gardens can be the most ornamental and lushly planted areas on campus with plants especially chosen for their thematic, aesthetic and aromatic qualities as well as shade to emulate a 'garden oasis.'
• Consider strategies to maintain the courtyard in an easy, consistent manner

Sustainable/green building design would seem a natural fit for the promotion of the use of outdoor spaces for education. The Leadership in Energy and Environmental Design (LEED) certification for Schools is the premier standard by which sustainable buildings are judged. The Innovation in Design category allows LEED points to be gained by using the school as a teaching tool. Several goals in the rating system support the notion of creating the highest quality learning environments.

One architectural method of achieving some of these LEED points is by providing courtyards. Courtyards provide more exterior wall surface and more exterior areas that provide views from the classrooms. Students, instead of being sequestered in an interior block of rooms with no natural light and no views, could enjoy daylight in their classrooms with views to rest their eyes and minds. The application of a courtyard theme could solve daylighting issues and at the same time provide a vital school component like an outdoor environmental learning area with many uses and forms.

Courtyards provide ways to add points to the LEED scoring:
• Protecting/restoring a habitat can be easily accomplished in courtyards
• Courtyards can add to open space calculations
• Some of the requirements of Quality and Quantity of Stormwater can be managed through the use of a courtyard by providing areas for stormwater best management practices (BMP's)
• Courtyards can be designed providing ponds or fountains and/or shade to promote natural convection to occur to alleviate the heat island effect
• By consciously choosing native plants, points may be gained in the water efficient landscaping category
• Providing cisterns that collect water from downspouts from the roof can provide water use reduction by capturing the water for later use in irrigation
• Courtyards are great places for solar arrays and other types of energy creating devices, meeting renewable energy and green power credits
• Materials reuse – bricks, tires, etc. could add to the quantity requirement of reusing materials to attain a credit
• Recycled content materials can be used in the courtyard such as Trex decking, patio furniture, picnic tables, and cob construction
• Using materials that come from less than 500 miles from the site can count toward points for regional materials
• By virtue of using courtyards, more light is provided to more rooms in the building. This allows classroom lights to be put on sensors, daylight and views are provided to add more points to the LEED calculation
• The courtyard can be designed to use the building itself as the teaching tool

6.2 Educational Garden

At times, building a garden can be overwhelming because of all the choices available

Figure32 Since completion, the Perry Schoolyard has become a well-used outdoor learning and recreation resource for the school community and neighbourhood.

in regards to plants, styles and designs. The best way to manage all these possible choices is to create a solid garden plan that includes a clear theme, design, plant catalogue and task list.

To succeed, an educational garden must first be created to:
• Tie into children and youth's interests
• Reflect the school's culture as shaped by administration, teachers, parents and neighbours
• Take into consideration the availability for maintenance by grounds crew, families, neighbours and volunteers. After having preliminary conversations with the various groups that will participate in the garden's development, care and maintenance, it is time to take all the collected ideas, recommendations, opinions and comments to create a draft design of the future garden. In an educational setting, a garden is most beneficial when thought of as an outdoor classroom where structured learning can be paired with experiential opportunities. (Figure 32)
The most successful outdoor classrooms tend to include:

6.2.1 Entrance (with gateway & fencing)
Gateway marks a clear transition from the schoolyard recess or play space-slowing the pace upon entering the outdoor classroom. A gateway designed so the user needs to change behaviour, perhaps squeeze through to enter, provides a unique kinesthetic cue that one is entering into a special place. Surrounding fence defines the outdoor classroom as special place for teaching and learning, and a unique living habitat in need of care and protection.

All outdoor classrooms are fully enclosed by fencing:
• to safely contain student activities- class management
• to protect site & plant materials from vandalism & outside activity, and prevent use by dogs
A signature gateway created by an artist provides unique identity for the outdoor classroom.

Considerations:
• *Lockable gate option (during out of school time, of recess if needed)*
• *Fully fenced area (consider appropriate height)*
• *Safety considerations- protecting students from vehicular areas (bollards)*
• *Consider integration of gateway with existing perimeter fence*
• *Reflect education themes-utilize a range of natural and people made materials*
• *Opportunity for gateway artwork project- aesthetically pleasing, whimsical, unique*
• *Material choice: functional, durable and sustainable (use heavy gage fence posts, connectors, locust wood, etc.) (Figure 33)*

6.2.2 Plants
It is recommended that any design for a campus garden should include a mix of three basic types of plants:
• Native Flowers: Plants that are both native to the region and also attract/support local pollinators
• Edibles: Predominantly fruits and vegetables but can include other edible plants
• Herbs: Mainly leafy plants that are used for flavour, aroma and healing properties

6.2.3 Seating
Seating provides clear locations for teacher to assemble and orient students upon entering the outdoor classroom.

Considerations
• *A variety of seating configurations ensures that students can easily work together as a full class, in small groups, or individually*
• *Dispersed seating allows students to choose to focus on different landscape features, locate in sun or shade, and have a variety of engaging experiences both with and separate from classmates*
• *Use a variety of different natural materials for seating elements, consider*

*educational and experiential value-soft/hard; rough /smooth; metamorphic /
igneous; warm/cool, etc.*
• Place seating so use does not conflict with planted areas (Figure 34)

6.2.4 Themes

Organizing the design of the garden around a theme, or multiple themes, is a
strong way of connecting to curricula, students' interests, etc. Some themes to
consider: historic/cultural garden. Throughout the world and through history,
various types of garden styles have been developed for aesthetic or functional
purposes. An educational garden can incorporate these styles into a design making
the garden a resource for social studies and other subject learning (examples:
Colonial Heirloom Garden, Three Sisters Garden or French Potager Garden).

Edible/Culinary Garden: These gardens provide students with hands-on
knowledge of food growing plants, an opportunity for understanding culturally
significant plants and their uses, and the opportunity to create materials out of
plant parts. Edible gardens can also include common herbs and vegetables that
allow students to grow, harvest and cook their own locally grown organic food.

Considerations
• Select species native to the region that produce edible fruit or nuts
*• Select annual and perennial herbs that students can use for cooking and general
tasting experience*
*• Incorporate culturally significant plant species that were traditionally used for
food and medicinal purposes*
*• Select species such as goldenrod that can be used for dye-making, and include
grasses, reeds and willows for basket making*

Sensory Garden: Especially good for younger children and as therapeutic tools,
these gardens use plants and design elements to create opportunities for
exploration using the five senses separately and/or combined.

35

Considerations
- *Include plants with smooth or rough leaves or bark for texture*
- *Include plants with fragrant fruit or flowers, or plants that emit an odour when their leaves are crushed (e.g. herbs)*
- *Include plants with colourful fruit, flowers, leaves and bark*
- *Include plants that have edible fruits and leaves for children to explore*
- *Provide sound from a number of trees, shrubs, wildflowers and reeds. Imagine the creak of a pine tree, the whispering of grass or the rustling of maple and aspen leaves in the fall*

Container Garden: Especially useful where space is limited, this method focuses on growing plants exclusively in containers. Containers can range from pots to specially built grow bags or recycled materials such as bathtubs and tires.

Art/Studio Garden: An art or studio garden in an educational setting is an outdoor gallery where students' work is incorporated and highlighted. Artwork can be inspirational, inviting and/or educational, heightening visitors' experiences. (Figure 35)

Rainbow garden: It's a colourful addition to campus.

Considerations:
- *Select plants with flowers that match the colours in a rainbow. Consider using white flowers to separate the colour sections and add contrast*
- *Include stepping stones and mosaic tiles that add colour and interest and provide a passage to the end of the rainbow*

Rooftop Garden: Rooftops are one of our cities' greatest untapped resources. They account for hundreds of acres of empty, under-utilized space, contributing to problems like the 'heat island effect' and increased storm water run-off. But rooftops could easily be turned into valuable green spaces, by creating green roofs of wildflowers, trees and shrubs or vegetables on schools, apartments, homes and places of work throughout the city.

Considerations
- *Calculate the loading capacity of the roof*
- *Plan for drainage from rainfall and from watering plants*
- *Plan for access to the roof membrane for maintenance and repair*
- *Choose the right plants for the rooftop garden*

Spiral Garden: The spiral is symbolic of a journey of discovery. The spiral can be a path, leading to a destination or to a point of discovery within the garden. Spiral gardens also control traffic on school grounds as students slow their speed to maneuver through the spiral.

Considerations
- *Create a pathway to easily lead you through the spiral*
- *Incorporate a variety of plant types to explore and interact with. Arrange the plants within plots throughout the spiral to create mini-gardens*
- *Use signs and directions to personalize and animate the space*
- *Arrange plants by themes to create a journey or to tell a story. For instance, a journey can be created through a meadow of wildflowers to an edge habitat of shrubs and wildflowers, and then to the forest so student experience different types of habitats*

Bird Seed Garden

Considerations
- *Plant seed from a bag of wild birdseed in the spring, covering the seed with two centimetres of soil. Water lightly but thoroughly to help the seeds germinating*
- *Provide birdhouses, perches and feeders in the garden to allow for natural seed distribution from birds*

Below is a chart listing a range of ideas for theme gardens. They provide ideas about the purpose and focus for the campus design.

Alphabet garden	Alpine garden	Annual garden	Art/Studio garden	Bee hive garden	Bird Seed garden
Bog garden	Butterfly garden	Carolina Fence garden	Container garden	Cut flower garden	Desert garden
Edible/Culinary garden	Ethnic garden	Ethnobotany garden	Fall garden	Gigant plant garden	Memorial garden
Moonlight garden	Music garden	Native plant garden	Organic garden	Peace garden	Pizza-shaped garden
Rain garden	Rainbow garden	Rooftop garden	Scarecrow garden	Sensory garden	Spiral garden
Spring garden	Storybook garden	Summer garden	Sunken Gardens	Tea garden	Vegetable garden
Vertical garden	Wetland Park	White garden	Wildlife habitat garden	Winter garden	Xeriscape Garden

Figure36 Due to the children's need for movement with a lot of possibilities to climb, jump and slide on it, or to be a conqueror in one of the integrated seats, the construction of playground equipment is made of steel to give maximum strength and durability.

6.3 Playgrounds

Playgrounds are areas on the school site designated for outdoor games and recreation and include play structures, paved play areas, open grassy areas, football fields, baseball fields, running tracks, etc. The playground is important not only because kids love to play, but because it is critical to their health and development, physically, mentally and emotionally, which will have a direct impact on the education. The most important thing to remember in planning a playground is the safety of the children. All Playground equipment must be well maintained regularly and the playground area kept clean of any broken glass or other dangerous debris. (Figure 36)

Guideline:
• Wherever possible spaces should be designed to be flexible and adaptable for use during different functions or by groups at different times
• Designs should consider culturally, architecturally and historically sensitive features, colours and textures that reflect the community and regional context
• Separate playgrounds from streets and parking lots
• Arrange playgrounds and athletics fields with easy access by maintenance trucks, spectators and/or community users
• Playgrounds should be well drained and free of holes, debris, poison plants, rocks, and other hazards which may lead to accidents
• Bury all anchoring devices below playing surfaces to eliminate tripping
• Retaining walls should be highly visible and elevation changes obvious
• Avoid cables, wires, ropes or flexible components in high-traffic areas
• All fasteners, connecting, and covering devices should not loosen or be removable without the use of tools and should have a corrosion-resistant coating
• Locate playgrounds and athletic fields near gym or classroom buildings for safe/easy access by the students, but not so close that it disrupts the classrooms environment

- Provide good separation between quiet and active play, as well as between play for different age groups
- Provide access to natural or wooded parts of sites whenever possible
- Surround the playground with non-toxic plants or fencing to prevent small children from inadvertently running into a street or leaving the playground unsupervised
- Solid surface playground surfacing is recommended for ease of maintenance, resiliency and durability where loose fill surfacing cannot be regularly maintained
- Keep playgrounds and athletic fields away from on-site sewage waste disposal systems and nitrification fields
- Provide shade features on east, west and south sides of play areas
- The design and layout of these secure external play areas should ensure that there are no hidden areas where the pupil is out of view of the supervising staff
- Disperse popular or heavy-use equipment to avoid crowding
- Locate moving equipment away from high activity areas
- Locate exits to slides in non-congested areas
- Play areas should accommodate students with special needs. Play areas should offer some stable paths paved with engineered wood, fibre, rubber mats or other material to access wheelchairs. Transfer stations on equipment will aid physically-challenged children to get off and on play structures. Wide paths, wheelchair parking spaces adjacent to the play areas, wider platforms and walkways help children using wheelchairs or crutches. The use of different textures and colours for paths and handrails can help visually-impaired children. Consideration should also be given towards the creation of a shaded outdoor area for pupils with photophobia. The surface of a playground may contain particles that may, in strong sunlight, make it dazzling for pupils with photophobia, and there is a need to assign a quiet area as well as an active area to prevent more active pupils knocking into more vulnerable pupils whilst playing.

6.4 Roads and Pathways

6.4.1 Major Roads
Major campus roads are defined as the primary vehicular routes around and through the campus. These include the ring road system and the major entrance routes to the campus.

Guideline:
• Major campus roads should be designed as parkways, with trees and landscaping lining the edges of the road
• Low impact traffic calming methods should be considered along major roads, including varying paving surfaces at important Intersections, roundabouts, neck downs at major pedestrian crossings and roadside landscaping. These traffic calming methods should be balanced by the need for efficient transportation movement, and other issues such as winter snow plowing and long term maintenance of the University's road system
• Roads should be designed to have minimum safe lane widths to encourage slower traffic speeds while still providing safe travel
• Allow for generous sight lines at intersections and at crosswalks. Do not install landscaping elements that will obscure sight lines
• Sidewalks should be provided along the entire length of road on at least one side, and on both sides of the road where possible
• Major roads should be separated from pedestrian paths by granite curbs and elevation changes
• Accommodations for bike lanes and other alternative transportation methods should be provided either within the road shoulders or immediately adjacent to the road

6.4.2 Minor Roads
Minor roads are those that provide access to the campus within the ring road, to campus parking lots and other destinations outside of the ring road. They are

characterized by one-or-two lane widths and slow speeds.

Guideline:
• Minor roads should be separated from pedestrian paths by granite curbs and elevation changes
• Road widths should be minimized to encourage reduced speeds while not sacrificing vehicular or pedestrian safety
• Traffic calming methods should be designed at regular intervals along minor roads, including crosswalk tables, varying paving surfaces near high-use pedestrian areas, neck downs and roadside landscaping

6.4.3 Major Pathways
A major pathway will be the primary desire line between two or more major destinations.

Often these paths will lead to the entrances of major buildings, to and from heavily used transportation centres like bus stops, large parking lots, and the parking garage, or be a conduit that provides links to many other paths. Major paths act as the spine of the pedestrian system.

Guideline:
• The width of any particular major path is a factor of the amount of traffic they accommodate and the scale of the landscape they intersect
• A walkway might need to double as a fire lane, in which case it should be widened appropriately
• The intersections of major pathways, especially those in the core campus area, should be emphasized and should accommodate seating areas, special plantings, and wayfinding elements
• Major paths should be concrete, with edges of a contrasting material. They should be designed to blend with other major campus paths to make a cohesive whole

- All major paths should accommodate the use of alternative wheeled transportation such as bicycles, roller blades and wheelchairs
- All major paths should be handicapped accessible, and should not have stairs
- Trash & recycling bins should be located along the path at regular intervals and at intersections of major paths
- Major paths should be well lit
- Paths should merge when approaching roads to condense the number of street crossings to a minimum. When major paths cross vehicular roads, it should always be at a right angle with an open view of the street
- If a bus stop is near a pedestrian street crossing, the crossing should be behind the parked bus if possible
- Service drives should not be alongside major paths. Similarly, service crossings of major paths should be minimized

6.4.4 Standard Pathways

Standard pathways accommodate fewer pedestrians than major pathways. They might connect a major destination with a minor destination, or lead to a major pathway, or to a secondary entrance of a building.

The campus landscape is currently crisscrossed with standard paths. Project designs should strive to reduce the number of paths where possible to clarify the means to reach one's destinations, as well as allow larger areas of landscaping. However, by minimizing the number of paths, it becomes more critical to evaluate the location of each path, maximizing its efficiency to reach the desired destination.

Guideline:
- Standard pathways should follow desire lines to their destinations. In cases where the desire line is not appropriate, an alternative route can be built with extensive landscaping features to encourage the use of the alternative route
- Most standard pathways will accommodate slower pedestrian speeds than major pathways, and the surrounding landscape should accommodate smaller, more

intimate scaled features
• Standard pathways should be well lit, using light poles having a height that is intimate in scale
• Stairs should be discouraged on standard pathways
• Standard pathways should accommodate trash & recycling bins near building entrances
• Where service drives intersect or parallel standard pathways, the service drive should be integrated into the design of the pathway while still maintaining adequate space for both functions to co-exist. Service vehicles should never park directly on pathways, but at designated service parking spaces located adjacent to standard paths with appropriate landscaping to minimize the negative visual effect to pedestrians

6.5 Plazas

Plazas function as paved areas for gatherings primarily in areas of heavy and frequent use. Plazas usually exist near building entrances, or at the intersections of major pathways. Plazas are an essential element to provide focus to the pedestrian experience. Plazas are generally hardscape, often contain seating, and are typically located adjacent to building entrances. These spaces are usually multi-use and their paved surfaces make them adaptable for a variety of activities. The design of plazas should be appropriate for the desired activity – sheltering trees or shrubs located close together to slow down traffic and provide quiet areas, open paved areas for large rallies, and benches in areas for resting and talking in smaller groups. These various activities can possibly occur within one plaza if the space is large enough to accommodate it and a hierarchy of use is well defined.

Guideline:
• Clear definition of space can be accomplished through plantings, seating, elevation changes, or other landscape elements
• The ability to move through plazas is an important design element and should be based on the desired primary activity

37

• The relationship between the plaza and the surrounding buildings and significant landscape features should be an important consideration in the design (Figure 37)
• Stairs should be minimized on plazas
• Views to and from plazas should be accommodated in the design
• Texture of plaza surfaces should be used to define space and suggest intended activity
• Sculpture or other 'hard' elements should be interactive and stimulating
• Seating arrangements should consider a variety of activities – intimate discussions, people-watching, quiet studying, group gatherings
• The design should consider the microclimate of the area, including sun exposure and seasonal conditions
• Plantings can be an effective means to bring human scale and intimacy to a plaza, as well as defining space and providing shade
• Plaza should be a well-lit and attractive space in the evenings as well as the daytime
• On large open plazas, power should be provided for occasional outdoor event
• An appropriate number of trash & recycling bins should be located in strategic places around the plaza

6.6 Surface Parking Lots

Intent
Adequate parking for staff and visitors must be considered as part of the site planning, especially in urban areas subject to high crime, but should be subordinate to children's needs for outdoor activity in those cases where sufficient land acquisition or design constraints does not allow for optimal creation of both schoolyards and parking.

Parking lots should be screened to minimize their visual impact on campus, but still provide safe access and egress and allow good surveillance and monitoring. Planting in surface parking lots can visually segregate the expanse of asphalt and shade pavements and vehicles.

Guidelines
- Parking lots should be designed to utilise as far as the possible the existing site access roads or in a new school the access road to the main entrance. Spaces should be designed in a cost-effective manner.
- Parking lots should be located adjacent to the staff and visitor entrances to the school. If a separate staff entrance is provided, the location of this access should be convenient to the car park. Separate car parks for staff and visitors are not recommended.
- Parking lots could be paved in a pervious material such as porous asphalt or open-grid pavers to permit water percolation into the ground, with concrete curbs where feasible
- Minimize scale of surface lots
- Large lots will be replaced with parking structures as the campus grows
- Lots should be designed with drainage detention swales for stormwater runoff interception and filtration
- Consider facilities for electric auto recharging where feasible
- Provide perimeter landscape buffers, designed to allow surveillance of the lot by campus security
- Designate a minimum of 10% of the parking area's interior for landscaping to enhance safety and comfort
- Each tree should be centred on at least 40 square feet of pervious soil area to ensure adequate air and water for root systems
- Lots should be shaded with trees to reduce excessive heat buildup. To increase shade, canopy trees should be provided every eight (8) linear stalls. Trees should be placed to minimize visibility conflicts. Planting islands should be staggered or triangulated to maximize the shade benefit from trees
- Low-maintenance trees should be used
- Provide clear and safe pedestrian circulation within surface lots
- Curb stops should be used sparingly

6.7 Planting

Campus plantings play a critical supporting role in shaping successful campus spaces and connections. Plantings can be arranged on a campus to provide color, scent, form and texture. They can be formal or more naturalistic, and they often help to divert and manage stormwater. There are various methods of greening campus such as by means of groves, landscape gardens, lawns, shrubberies, garden plots, container plants, and the use of planters, trellised and hanging baskets. The health and maintenance level of those plantings and lawns are essential to providing campus with a high quality image.

Sustainability
• Minimize irrigation through the selection of plants appropriate to specific campus environments and use
• The use of turf requires more irrigation and care on high-use areas such as courtyards and malls with a walkable surface
• Utilize native or climate-appropriate plantings
• Promote water conservation by using a computer-regulated irrigation system as well as efficient subterranean drip irrigation systems

General Guidelines
• Primary considerations should be healthy plant growth and ease of maintenance
• Provide adequate soil and growing space for plant material
• Respect and reinforce natural and designed planting patterns and the intrinsic character and recognizable order of the campus
• Locate trees to maximize exposure to winter sun and provide summer shade
• Consider fragrance, sound, colour and texture in planting design (Figure 38)
• Certain trees having unusual characteristics or distinctive features may be planted as a focal point in the landscape, but this situation should be minimized so as not to reduce the impact of other focal trees on the campus
• All trees and shrubs shall be non-invasive species

• To reduce maintenance needs, the campus encourages the use of plants that do
not require heavy ongoing pruning and that are not likely to snag unsightly trash
• Trees should not be planted within 10 feet of steam lines, electric lines, water,
sewer or drainage lines
• Trees or shrubs that produce fruit should be located far enough from pedestrian
sidewalks that the fruit does not fall on sidewalks

38

6.7.1 Streetscape Planting

Streetscapes, formal gateways and dropoffs should be aesthetically and functionally reinforced with street trees and median plantings.

Guidelines
- Plantings are to be wayfinding cues to guide pedestrians sequentially through campus
- Street trees should be adequately spaced, depending on species, to provide shade and cooling for pedestrians and reduce the overall urban heat island effect
- Trees should have low maintenance requirements and sufficient hardiness to withstand the region's hot climate and the effects of adjacent traffic
- Where possible, planting strips (or 'parkways') for street trees should be added between new sidewalks and road edges
- Consider using structural soil in sidewalk and planting strip areas (for large trees) to minimize soil compaction and encourage healthy tree growth

6.7.2 Building-specific Planting

Guidelines
- Select plants for their colour, texture, scent, seasonal change and shade
- Consider the use of perennials and flowering trees to create focal areas where appropriate
- Select trees and plants that will look their best throughout the academic year
- Consider plants related to a specific building's academic programmes or function
- Provide root barriers for courtyard trees and trees adjacent to hardscape to minimize pavement damage

6.7.3 Structural Planting

The campus landscape includes 'structural' plantings of trees, shrubs and groundcovers adjacent (and sometimes attached) to buildings and walls that

Figure.39 Stamford Environmental Magnet School

provide important form and edges to the campus setting. Structural planting helps to blend buildings into the campus, provides screening of utility and service areas and directs pedestrian movement to building entries.

Guidelines
• Utilize a simple palette of mass plantings that provides uniformity and consistency throughout the campus
• Provide safety and visibility while establishing a cohesive and uniform aesthetic
• Provide accent plantings at key building entries
• Consider using evergreen plants for year-round shade and on north-facing areas. Focus deciduous trees on south-facing areas, to allow for winter sun and summer shade
• Consider including large tree species as vertical punctuation between buildings and to provide shade

6.8 Stormwater Management

Stormwater management features can provide aesthetic and educational benefits in addition to controlling the quantity and quality of runoff. Some methods to convey and infiltrate the water include bioretention swales and ponds, runnels, and permeable pavements. (Figure 39)

6.8.1 Considerations
• Where possible the design should maintain and enhance natural drainage patterns, especially arroyos
• Design for natural infiltration and evaporation where possible to reduce water run-off during storm events
• Bioswales incorporated into school parking lot designs provide an opportunity to improve the water quality and reduce the amount of runoff

6.8.2 Case Study

Figure40 Ohlone Community College

The grading, drainage, and utilities of the Ohlone Newark College Campus were designed not only to convey runoff off-site, but also to slow and cleanse stormwater prior to discharge. Rather than 'hard-piping' runoff directly to the discharge point, the storm drainage system utilized various landscape-based and mechanical elements that were incorporated into the site and landscape design meant to reduce pollutants in stormwater flowing off-site. (Figure40)

The Ohlone College storm drainage system actually consists of two independent systems that ultimately feed into a large vegetated swale/retention pond south of the campus. The system was split in two to separate relatively 'clean' runoff from roof, site hardscape, and landscaping areas from 'dirty' water coming from parking lots and vehicular access areas.

The storm drainage system installed in the centre of the College collects runoff from the main building roof, landscaping areas, and site hardscaping surrounding the building. Much of the site hardscape drains to landscaping areas prior to being collected by area drains, which effectively filters out suspended solids and allows much of the dissolved organics and phosphorous to be removed by natural biological processes. Roof downspouts were allowed to directly connect to the underground system as no significant introduced chemicals were anticipated from roof runoff. After being collected by downspouts and area drains, runoff is transported via an underground pipe to a vegetated swale aptly nicknamed the 'stormwater garden' due to the visible stormwater flow in this area and the natural grasses and vegetation. The 'stormwater garden' further filters and cleanses runoff prior to collection and discharge into the large swale /retention pond south of the site.

The storm drainage system installed at the periphery of the campus collects runoff from the two major parking lots, landscape islands, and drive aisles. Additional BMP measures were provided for runoff from this system due to the increased potential for suspended solids and toxins. Bioswales were incorporated along the east and west property lines to provide suspended solids and chemical removal for drive aisles. To further aid in pollutant removal, two hydrodynamic separators were installed immediately upstream of the large retention pond to capture suspended solids. As a tertiary measure, discharge from the hydrodynamic separators was directed to two sedimentation ponds that spill into the large swale /retention pond.

Both on-site systems collecting runoff from the Campus discharge into a large vegetated retention basin that extends approximately 900 feet to the south. After passing through the stormwater garden, hydrodynamic separators, and sedimentation basins, stormwater flows through this long grassed channel that further filters out suspended solids. Being fully planted year-round, the swale also serves as a biological filter that reduces dissolved toxins and chemicals such as nitrogen and phosphorous which have the potential to cause eutrophication in local streams and the San Francisco Bay. The primary discharge point of the retention pond is through a 12inches restrictive outlet pipe that limits the flow such that stormwater is stored during heavy storms, reducing the potential for downstream flooding and bank erosion.

Through careful site planning with stormwater quality in mind, the designers of the Ohlone Newark Campus delivered a product that was not only functional but aesthetically pleasing as well.

6.9 Lighting

Effective lighting is a necessary part of any campus to provide security but it can also be used to enhance an environment, adds to the night-time vitality of campus. The style of the light fixture can provide character and help create a unique identity to spaces. Used uniformly, lighting can contribute to a sense of place on campus.

Figure 41 The plaza, which is in use 24 hours a day, seven days a week, incorporates several layers of lighting, which reduce to lower levels after midnight.

Lighting should focus on providing an even, consistent coverage, softening contrast ratios at edges and thus improving visibility by avoiding excess illumination and brightness. Campus lighting should also be well-organized in simple patterns which reinforce the open space, courtyards and plazas and circulation on campus. (Figure 41)

Sustainability
• Light illuminating from fixtures should be cast downward with full cut-off shades
• Specify lighting for maximum durability, energy-efficiency and lifespan
• Use minimum lighting levels required by code and campus standards; focus on contrast ratios versus standard foot-candle light levels

General Guidelines
• Provide sufficient lighting to establish safe conditions for access and circulation
• Building entrances and campus wayfaring signs should all be well lit
• Consider lighting to enhance the aesthetic qualities of the campus and highlight special features and trees at night
• In-ground up-lighting should be avoided to minimize maintenance and vandalism
• Coordinate lighting locations and pole heights with tree locations and landscape areas and constructed elements
• Plants should not interfere with the effectiveness of the lighting.

6.9.1 Free-standing Lighting

Intent
Consistent pedestrian lighting is an important contributor to the identity of the campus and can help suggest a hierarchy of travel routes.

Guidelines

Figure42 The designers thought to include the joy of finding in the landscape. So they hoped that students feel the regularity of arrangement of furniture and trees, and the order of commonality in materials and form, and natural providence. They tried to design the pavement and furniture which make students feel something significant with the years.

• Walks and paths should be uniformly illuminated
• Parking areas, pedestrian plazas, campus building entries, loading areas and courtyards should be illuminated
• Pole spacing should be determined by pole height, luminaire type and desired foot candles
• Pole placement should reinforce the linearity of campus open space and circulation

6.9.2 Building Lighting

Intent
Building-specific light fixtures can be integral components of buildings, highlighting significant features and identifying entries.

Guidelines
• Lights should be compatible with buildings and should articulate and accent their landscape context
• Lighting should be indirectly focused. Light sources should not be visible
• Consider the additive effect of spilled light from building interiors when placing exterior fixtures

6.10 Furnishings

Furnishings are important elements of the exterior public realm. They help define the campus character and improve the livability and comfort of outdoor spaces by providing places to gather, study and socialize, thus improving collegial communication and interaction. Furnishings should be selected and located to maintain the cleanliness and order of campus and enhance circulation. (Figure 42)

Figure43 Bares Alumni Walk is composed of two parallel walks. Seating groupings perpendicular to the long walk are formed by parallel bars of precast seats with integrated lighting. These same precast elements are utilized in the amphitheatre/outdoor campus.

Furnishings on major campus malls should match the existing palette of simple concrete pieces. Non-standard furnishings should be replaced. In all other campus spaces, different pieces are permitted as long as they recognize the distinct character of adjacent buildings and meet the guidelines. This consistency and contextual consideration both enhances the campus's image and can help reduce maintenance costs.

Sustainability
Selection of furnishings should consider:
• Local climate
• Recycled content
• Durability and lifespan
• Minimizing the use of toxic materials (paints, finishes, glues)

General Guidelines
Furnishings should be:
• Efficient to repair and maintain
• Vandal-resistant
• Selected in coordination with campus lighting, signage and buildings
• Located to avoid conflicts with site maintenance
• Located to take advantage of shade

6.10.1 Benches/seating

Intent
In highly-public areas, seating can serve to invite collegial group activities, dining and informal study or introspection. A variety of comfortable seating along walks, paths, courtyards and plazas is an important contributor to the pedestrian circulation system. A family of benches should encompass a range of seating requirements. (Figure 43)

Figure44 There is a difference in height between play area and schoolyard, so a small wall made of individual concrete elements was created – and by fixing some red and sunny-yellow seats on it this wall developed as a sitting wall for the children to talk to each other or for balancing over it.

Guidelines
• Provide seating throughout campus, particularly in the following areas:
  Plazas and courtyards, especially those offering shade;
  Building entries;
  Along major and minor pedestrian walks;
  Oriented toward interesting and varied views;
  Near transit stops, with a clear view of approaching buses.
• Incorporate fixed seating at a comfortable height into planters, low dividing walls and the facades of buildings where appropriate as an alternative to stand-alone benches (Figure 44)
• Group benches and trash receptacles as a composition of elements for practicalities of usage and to reduce visual clutter
• Locate seating to take advantage of public activities, views, sun in winter and shade in summer and shelter from the wind
• Provide some seating for individual, introspective use
• Ensure compatibility with the architectural and landscape setting
• All benches or seat walls should utilize creative prevention measures to reduce or eliminate damage from skateboarders and cyclists. Armrests are suggested to deter skateboarding
• Benches with backs are preferred for comfort

6.10.2 Tables and Chairs

a. Moveable

Intent
The use of moveable tables and chairs can allow for dynamic seating arrangements and can encourage more active use of campus gathering spaces. Such furniture can be moved to allow for more comfortable seating locations and to accommodate different group sizes. This flexibility allows spaces to be cleared for special events. This type of seating is well-suited for dining and is also particularly popular for

informal outdoor study sessions. (Figure45)

Guidelines
• Consider moveable tables and chairs in areas of high public use and visibility
• Tables in open, un-shaded areas should include a shade umbrella. Umbrellas should be made from UV-resistant fabric that repels mildew and stains and is resilient to power-washing
• Moveable furniture must be managed and supervised to minimize damage or theft

b. Stationary

Intent
Stationary tables and chairs are typically picnic table type units. They can serve to define spaces as gathering areas, particularly for outdoor dining. Seating should be planned to provide a variety of sun/ shade conditions and seat combinations. (Figure 46)

Guidelines
• Tables and chairs should be simple as well as architecturally and aesthetically appropriate
• Tables in open, un-shaded areas should include a shade umbrella
• Choose units that allow for wheelchair user access
• Locate seating to discourage inappropriate use by skateboarders, or other activities unrelated to seating or dining

6.10.3 Campus Art
Public campus artwork provides special identity to campus, and signals that the area is unique, cared for and valued. It's the most sustainable of schoolyard elements and contributes to respect for the site. Artists working in collaboration with the landscape architect are able to create artwork that is integrated into the

site design, examples: gateway, fencing, seating, or paving patterns. (Figure47)
Considerations
• Content options: historic, cultural expression, playful, abstract colour, memorial, etc.
• A variety of mediums - metal, clay, murals, mosaics, concrete
• Wide cost range – from painted murals by volunteers to cast bronze sculpture requiring footings by a contractor
• Installation of artworks requires an approval process (site owner, City Art Commission, funders)
• Consider including space for performing arts – poetry, music, small classroom performances

Figure47 The landscape architect worked together with San Francisco artist Anna Valentina Murch to incorporate a carved granite bubbler at the head of the water channel and stainless steel spiral shapes imbedded into porous glass paving designed to evoke images of raindrops.

48

Guidelines
• Select art that relates to associated academic programmes to enhance the learning experience
• Placement of each art piece should relate to its immediate surroundings and context within the campus
• Art should be vandal-resistant and should not require extensive on-going maintenance
• Art can be used functionally as an element of site furnishings

6.10.4 Bicycle Parking

Guidelines
• Bicycle parking should be visible, accessible and safe, day and night. Provide shade and shelter where possible
• Provide sufficient bike racks to avoid unsightly random parking, based on projected use of adjacent building
• Provide covered, secure and lighted bicycle parking in all parking garages
• Consider providing bike lockers to commuters
• Provide covered, secure and lighted bicycle parking at every new residence hall. Retrofit older halls to provide such facilities where possible. (Figure48)

Bicycle Racks
Bike racks are generally placed near building entrances for ease of use. Bike racks can be part of a site furnishing family to help create a consistent style throughout campus.

Intent
Bicycle racks are important elements of the campus circulation system and their effective use can help to promote alternative transportation methods.

Guidelines

• Choose secure racks that function well but also look aesthetically pleasing when no bikes are present
• Existing campus standard ribbon rack or single U-loop racks should be consistently installed in areas adjacent to building entries. The finish should be either powder-coated (patrician bronze) or stainless steel (determined by project and location) and installed by embed whenever feasible
• Other than the ribbon racks at building entrances, a specific style of bicycle rack is not recommended as aesthetic tastes change and designs for security and durability evolve regularly
• When locating racks near building entries, ensure the racks do not interrupt the flow of pedestrians into the building
• Racks should allow an entire bicycle to be locked, not just one wheel

6.10.5 Bollards

Intent
Bollards are short vertical posts used to define a perimeter or create a low barrier between vehicular and pedestrian traffic. They can also provide light or decoration and are sometimes removable for occasional vehicular access.
The need for vehicles to enter the campus via pedestrian routes should first be minimized through careful site design. Minimize over-use of bollards, which can impede pedestrian flow.

Guidelines
• Removable bollards are appropriate where service and emergency vehicles require temporary access to the pedestrian/ bicycle only routes. Contact the Campus Fire Marshal before selecting removable bollards to determine type and location
• Bollard design should be simple in design, architecturally and aesthetically appropriate and should complement other site furnishings

Figure50 The existing population of trees were integrated into the setting and gave off shade on hot days.

6.10.6 Shading devices

Shading devices can be broken down into two groups – natural and man-made. Natural is easy – usually trees or some large shrubs are the best way to provide shade. The disadvantage of this technique is that in new construction it takes years for a newly planted tree or shrub to attain a height and size large enough to provide adequate shade. Most likely the easy solution, whether on a temporary or permanent basis, is to consider providing man-made shading devices until natural ones grow into their task. (Figure49)

Architecturally designed structures can provide shade and define space. The materials that can be used are limitless - wood, metal, or fabric are a few common materials. Trellises and arbours built along a wall are a good example of this type of shading device. Deeper arbours and trellis structures should be used to shade the east and west sides of the building. A space of 1-6 inches should be left between the building and any vine covered screen in order to allow ventilation and cooling.

49

Figure49 Large umbrellas provide shade for the upper terraces

Colourful fabric structures with playful forms may also be integrated into the courtyard design to provide shade. The structures can act as focal points or gathering spaces within the courtyard. Gazebos and small structures can also be built within the courtyard to define different areas of use. Ensure that all structures are accessible, providing either no stairs for entry or an accessible ramp if elevated. A firm, level, stable, slip resistant path must be provided.

Strategically placed trees can provide shade. (Figure 50) Plantings also improve air quality by filtering pollutants. In order to make the most use of the properties of the different types of trees, place deciduous vines or trees toward the north and evergreen trees to the east and west. The deciduous trees will shed their leaves and allow the winter sun to enter any window openings into the building. Carefully study the canopy of the tree as it will also determine the spread of the roots. If a tree's canopy is 20 feet in diameter, the roots of the tree will also extend 10 feet in all directions from the trunk. Planting the tree too close to the building can cause damage to foundations or be a maintenance nuisance should leaves fall on the roof and clog drains. Be aware of and avoid utility and water lines in the area proposed to plant the tree. Always use native species.

Examples of shading devices:
• Canvas
• Wood trellises, pergolas, or arbours
• Metal canopies
• Roof overhangs
• Tensile fabric structures, tents
• Tree canopies

David de Wied Building

Completion date:
2011
Location:
Utrecht, the Netherland
Designer:
Willem Jan Snel, Maike van Stiphout (DS)
Photographer:
Willem Jan Snel
Client:
University of Utrecht Property Management & Campus
Area:
11,000m^2

Project description:

The faculty for natural sciences and engineering of the University of Utrecht has recently moved to a new home on the university campus called 'David de Wied' building. The campus ('De Uithof'), is an area in which many different partners strive to realise a first rate knowledgecentre within an urban plan designed by OMA. Important focal point in the urban plan is a high quality public space, for which DS is responsible throughout the Uithof. The new building, beautifully designed by Studio HH, is located on the edge of the central park, which is organised around an old stronghold dating from 1877. The concept behind the plan is to incorporate the new building inside the landscapepark by wrapping the grass around the

building and making it possible for the sheep (the 'gardeners' of the park) to walk almost right up to the building.

The main entrance is located on the first floor, 5 metres above the landscape. On the west side an open air lecture hall and a long, lazy access ramp accompanied by a custom designed handrail, negotiate the height difference between the central square on the first floor and the landscape below. On the sunny south side, the landscape slopes up toward the central square from which one can enjoy a beautiful view over the park. Large concrete strips, accompanied by benches, make the slope accessible and create a pleasant human scale. A dramatic overhang on the Universiteitsweg, the busiest street of De Uithof, not only makes this building an important

Site Plan

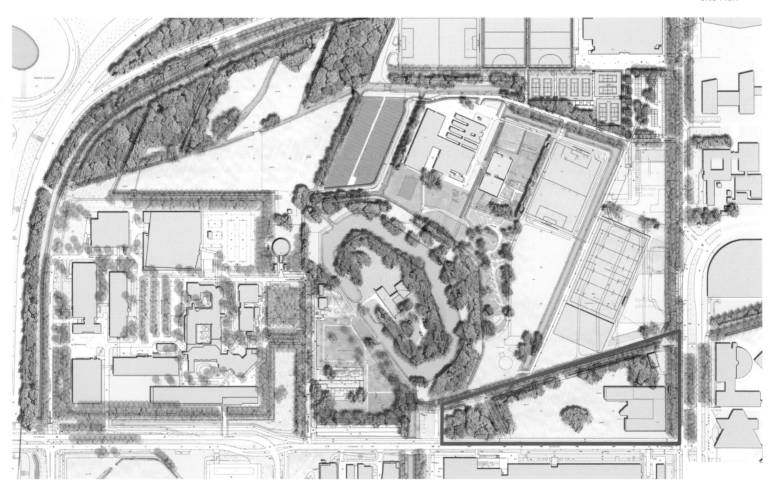

landmark, but also creates a large space to place the many bicyclestands required for a university campus. The landscape design creates a meaningful place for the new building within the urban tissue of the Uithof.

1. The building and a public square
2. The main entrance of the building is located on the first floor.
3. The green slope connected with the central square
4. Large cement belt and benches

5. An open air lecture hall on the west side
6. Bicycle stands
7-9. Landscape details

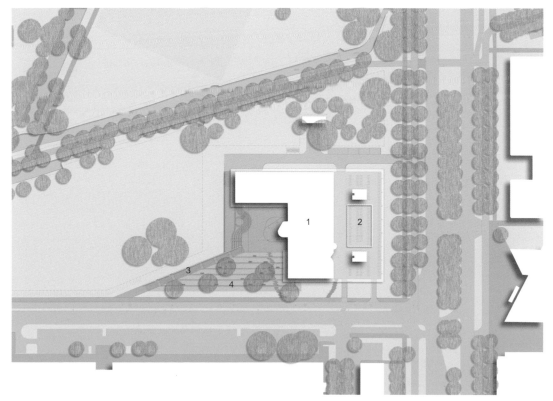

1. David de Wied Building
2. Bike Parking Area
3. Slope
4. Green Slope

Plan

Lavin Bernick Centre for University Life, Tulane University

Completion date:
2007
Location:
New Orleans, USA
Designer:
Coen + Partners
Photographer:
Paul Crosby
Area:
8,785 m²
Award name:
2010 ASLA-MN Yearly
Awards (American Society
of Landscape Architects,
Minnesota Chapter)

Project description:

The Lavin Bernick Centre at Tulane University includes the design of a pocket park and plaza connected to the redesign and expansion of the student centre by project lead Vincent James Associates Architects. Coen + Partners, intent for the exterior landscape surrounding the Centre was to create a vibrant heart for campus life by reconnecting the interior spaces of the building to the exterior while successfully knitting the site into the existing campus fabric; thus, the architecture and landscape had to work as one cohesive unit.

The landscape architect conducted extensive research on the best building practices to withstand constant fluxes in climate such as flooding, tropical storms, hurricane force winds, and extreme heat and humidity.

Research on the climatic conditions and best construction practices for this region was critically important to the outcome of this project. In addition, research into the design vernacular of New Orleans helped to prescribe a series of precepts for the landscape design. The design explores ways to convey the lushness of the semitropical New Orleans climate through refined form and texture.

The landscape spaces are designed to create great flexibility for a myriad of activities. This allows for multiple events to take place simultaneously without compromising the interconnectedness of the overall design. Gathering areas radiate from the building edge at grade creating a series of outdoor rooms while allowing for the boundaries of the building site to disappear. Structured elements such as large umbrellas provide shade for the

2

upper terraces while a crape myrtle bosque shelters the lower terrace and filters views from the street into the pocket park. Originally designed as a building façade treatment by the architect, Coen + Partners proposed extending vertical planes of climbing vines from the building into the surrounding landscape through the creation of custom vine screens. The insertions create soft divisions between passive and active spaces, providing filtered privacy for adjacent reading areas and variable levels of shading to help mediate extreme shifts of solar gain. The vines become a focal point for the pocket park and are an innovative solution for introducing native plants into the compact space.

Linear ipe wood and aluminum benches along thoroughfares and within the pocket park recall the horizontal façade treatment of the building. A nearly three-hundred foot long custom bench conceals a concrete flood wall protecting the lower level of the building from seasonal flooding.

1. Night view of the entrance
2. Crepe myrtle Bosque / lawn
3. The design of trees reflects the lushness of the semitropical climate.
4. The trees are surrounded by benches.

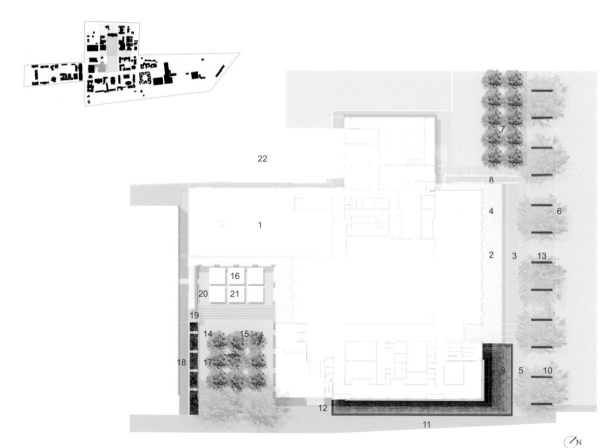

1. New university centre
2. Upper quad terrace
3. Quad staircase
4. Parasol
5. Campus walk
6. Ipe wood benches
7. Crepe myrtle bosque / lawn
8. Ada access ramp
9. Sloped garden area (to reveal basement level)
10. Custom bike racks
11. 270' bench / flood wall
12. Primary building entrance
13. Existing live oak trees
14. Custom vine screens
15. Lower pocket park terrace
16. Upper pocket park terrace
17. Vine reading rooms / seating
18. Ipe wood screen fence
19. Upper level stair access
20. Movie screen
21. Removable umbrellas
22. Service area

Site Plan

5. Custom made benches are provided around the building.
6. Boundary of the site is blurred under the long wood benches along the building and the vegetation.
7. Students in the rest area
8. The vines forms a screen, bringing a sense of privacy to the reading area
9. The climbing plants together with the supporting cables create a screen of vines.

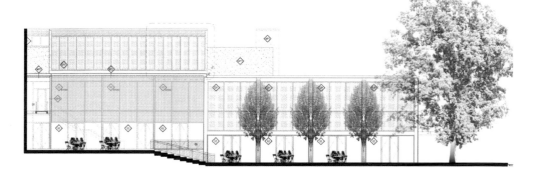

Sections

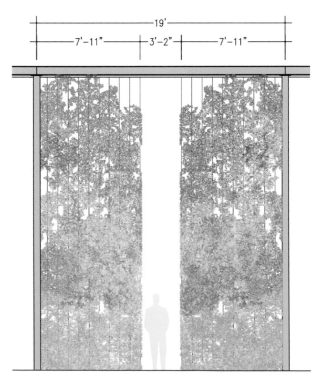

Vinewall-ELEV

9

Jardins Du Rolex Learning Centre – EPFL

Completion date:
2009
Location:
Lausanne, Switzerland
Designer:
Paysagestion architectes-paysagistes SIA
Area:
90,000m²

Project description:

The Rolex Learning Centre and its outdoor space create today's main access to the Federal Polytechnic Institute of Lausanne.The Federal Polytechnic Institute of Lausanne (EPFL) is one of the most innovative institutions in the world. Its current pace of development is spectacular: a scientific park, a hotel, student housing, a convention centre and the Rolex Learning Centre. The Rolex Learning Centre is conceived to have access to information in any format. It is also a public space for the interaction of people and scientific disciplines.

The complex has three different levels. There is an underground parking lot on top of which an open public space gives on to a garden. The public space is sheltered by an undulating and perforated roof. This roof is also the floor of a unique sloping level, generously lit by the large cell shaped patios.

A year before the inauguration of the Learning Centre (May 2010), the institute had launched a competition to link the new Learning Centre to the rest of the campus. The call for tender was addressed to general contractors and their affiliate subcontractors.

For the landscaping project, the affiliate subcontractors chose a contextual approach. EPFL's site is located on a small plain formed by moraine organic shaped ridges. This flat surface has an orthogonal geometry. Historically, on this surface, vegetable growing operation and then the built environment settled there.

The Learning Centre not only integrates the urban fabric (a large rectangle of 166x122 metres) but also its natural context: the moraine landscape (ripples and alveolar) and the lemanic landscape. Surrounding, the Learning Centre building, the gardens expresses the duality of this context (orthogonal campus, trail and

plantations). The flat topography is respected, with the exception of a gentle grass slope offering a picnic space.

The building is a little constrained in this densely built campus. To overcome this, a large meadow, and a few group of trees give the impression of larger open space. Four lines of variably dense trees, define the limits of this meadow. These tree-filters open up to the distant landscape and become denser near the buildings.

1. Aerial view of the whole campus
2. The complex has three different levels: an underground parking lot on top of which an open public space gives on to a garden.
3. Large lawn and trees
4. Lawns in front of the building
5. Trees become denser near the buildings.
6. Building being integrated to the surroundings

7. It also integrates its natural context: the
moraine landscape (ripples and alveolar)
and the lemanic landscape.
8. Place between the moraine landscape
and the lawns
9. Entrance of the campus
10. Details of the lawns

Rochester Institute of Technology (RIT) Global Plaza

Completion date:
2010
Location:
Rochester, USA
Designer:
SWA GROUP
Photographer:
Tom Fox
Area:
101,171m²

Project description:

RIT's Global Village is a new campus residential neighbourhood for 2,000 students that creates a new social heart for RIT – Global Plaza. The neighbourhood's strong pedestrian 'walk and courtyard' pattern extends RIT's walk and courtyard spine and provides seamless links to existing campus housing beyond. The project replaced rambling parking lot-centric townhouse clustered, tripling the number of students that can live in a sophisticated, active street scene adjacent to the academic core.

The neighbourhood's centrepiece – Global Plaza – creates a landmark place with a mosaic of dining, studying and socialising spaces including a permeable café zone and more-defined restaurant terrace with seating for over 300, a central outdoor lounge with resort-style deep seating, fire pit and trellis-framed performance area, and a south-facing conical lawn 'beach'

at the base of the curved Innovation Centre at the plaza's entrance. An internally-lit, faceted, patterned glass fountain located at the intersection of the plaza's pedestrian flows serves as a glowing landmark and meeting point year round.

The architects and landscape architects worked closely with the University to choreograph storefront and plaza uses to maximise the attractiveness of the plaza while balancing operational issues such as minimising kitchen duplication and providing convenient service and loading. The intimately-scaled plaza today is surrounded by six cafés and restaurants, a bar, an international food market, a convenience store, a wellness/fitness centre, a handmade gift and art shop, a hair salon, a copy shop and post office. The University's offices for Global Learning and flexible seminar and club rooms are located alongside the second level promenade.

The plaza includes elements to extend its use in Rochester's cool and cold weather during much of the school year, including user-operated timed gas heaters in the café seating zone, umbrellas for hot or drizzling days, and a fire pit in the central lounge. In the coldest months, the lounge is detailed so that it can be cleared, lined and flooded to transform into a small recreational skating rink. During warmer months, the University programmes the plaza with almost daily events including performances, festivals and student club and social events.

The landscape architects designed and selected all elements between building façades, including furniture and umbrellas, excepting campus standard pole lights and trash receptacles. The restaurant terrace includes subtle reuse of salvaged bollards from RIT's original campus in downtown Rochester. Large-growing canopy tree species, generally absent on campus, will over time reinforce Global Plaza as a landmark for RIT. Planting on the low, angled restaurant roof provides attractive views for residents above as well as modest additional habitat. A few simple geometries of evergreen boxwood hedges provide structure to the plaza through the winter.

The project's compact layout, pedestrian orientation, bicycle facilities, planted roof, distributed rain gardens and provision for summer shade contributed to the project's pending LEED Gold rating. The plaza, which is in use 24 hours a day, seven days a week, incorporates several layers of lighting, which reduce to lower levels after midnight.

Plan
1. Entrance from Academic Core
2. Café Zone
3. Central Promenade
4. Restaurant Terrace
5. Planted Roof
6. Iconic Fountain
7. Central Lounge
8. Stores around Plaza
9. Upper Terrace
10. Seat Stairs
11. Bike Parking
12. Hillside Student Housing

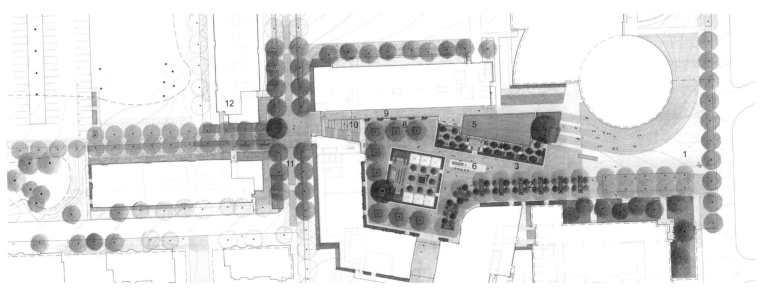

7

1. Entrance to Global Plaza, from RIT's academic core
2. Stores around Global Plaza, with seat stairs and upper terrace connecting to hillside student housing beyond
3. Lawn leading to Informal Café Zone adjacent to central promenade
4. Bicycle parking canopies along campus path/fire lane
5. Restaurant terrace along central promenade, with iconic glass fountain beyond
6. Central Lounge, with trellis and festival lights over small stage
7. Central Lounge, looking from side of small stage
8. Wood Trellis, detailed with plantation grown 38mm width Western Red Cedar

8

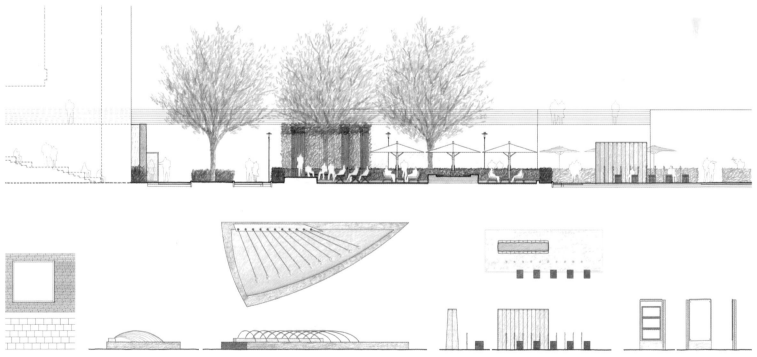

Design studies for Fountain

9. Central Lounge, with wood deck and moveable resort furniture

10. Central Lounge, with resort deep seating and central fire pit

11. Iconic Glass Fountain

12. Planted roof over low Restaurant pavilion

13. Bicycle parking canopies

14. Hillside student housing lobby entrance

15. Global Plaza preparation for opening day

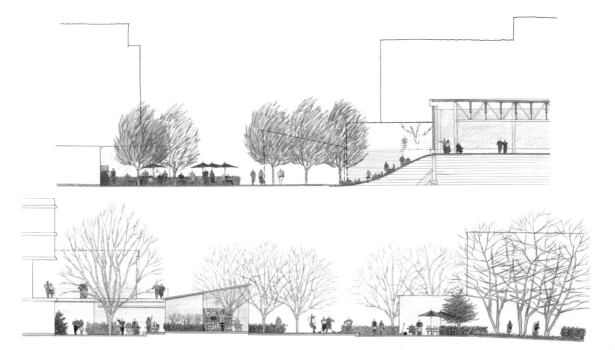

Design studies of hillside transitions and plaza width

Northwest Vista College

Completion date:
2010
Location:
San Antonio, USA
Designer:
SWA GROUP
Photographer:
SWA GROUP
Area:
607,028m²

Project description:

Northwest Vista College is situated in the oak covered hills west of San Antonio, with beautiful views to city and surrounding valley. This project design, building on SWA's master plan, seeks to sensitively integrate new buildings and associated roads and parking into the pristine oak covered hills that surround the campus, allowing for the preservation of existing trees and adding native plantings. A 2.5-acre lake situated in a natural ravine visually connects the two sides of the campus while providing for storm water detention requirements. Bio-filtration and Stillen basins will help to capture sediments and pollutants before releasing storm water flows into the natural drainage channels that exit the site.

The east side of the campus will be formed by a series of new buildings terraced up a gentle hillside and arranged around a sloped quadrangle. A new fine arts centre will anchor the upper portion of the quad, and serve as the architectural centrepiece of the campus as viewed from the lake below and the surrounding community.

Site Plan

1. Courtyard view from the lake
2. Island in the heart of the lake which has connected the two ends of the campus
3. Rest area on the lawn
4. S-shape paths and retaining wall planted with grass
5. Lawns, stone paths and stairs
6. Sunken plaza surrounded by rails
7. Garage and oak trees integrate together.

8. Lakeside stone roads, together with the grassland form a beautiful picture
9. The bridge is a fine connection of the campus' landscape elements.
10. Curve roads and the plants beside

Access area of Campus Nord at UPC University

Completion date:
2007
Location:
Barcelona, Spain
Designer:
taller 9s arquitectes (Oriol Cusidó & Irene Marzo, architects)
Photographer:
Adrià Goula Sardà
Area:
6,500m²
Awards:
V Rosa Barba Europea landscape prize 2008

Project description:

The objective of the intervention was to recover an existing 'terrain vague' to citizen usage, turning it into a new gate to UPC university in Barcelona. The area, was a 'closed' urban space, a great 'cut' in the physical relationship among the area of university buildings in the north and the pedestrian flows from south. The intervention solves the connectivity with closer urban environment and improves the accessibility to Campus creating new paths according existing flows.

The first objective was upholstering with green the most part of the area, offsetting the excess of paved zones in the Campus and offering a new space for leisure.

The second goal was to consider the set of diverse and separated elements that were in the area (the cover of the buried parking, the lineal

element of ventilation, the crooked walls which hide the gymnasium, the stairs to the Campus, topographic conditions, alignments...) whom are an inheritance of partial and autonomous former interventions, to gather them all in an unitary idea.

The third criteria was to avoid the idea of paths as an infrastructure to design ways that generate spaces of sociability. The different formalization of the 2 paths are consequence of the different relationship with the 'green' and with the pre-existences. The way from south it is formalized as a GROOVE that cuts the 'green', which opens up in the vegetal terrain. Through its organic definition creates small squares, where benches and trees are placed. The path is created through a series of concrete walls of variable height lined with plates of weathering steel, which solve the transition between the topography and the path, embracing the pre-existent elements and shaping soft slopes pending in south. On the

other hand, the pedestrian eastern path is conceived as a MAT placed on the cover of the parking. The mat is designed with prefabricated pieces of concrete placed on the existing cover and accompanied by a sinuous bench of concrete.

3

1. The access provides students a good placc to relax.
2. The way of the plaza is formalised as a groove.
3. Two different paths links up the green belt and other elements.

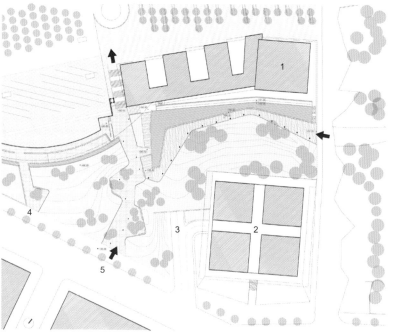

1. Omega building
2. Nexus building
3. Access to buried parking lot
4. Access to gymnasium
5. Jordi girona street

Site Plan

4. The path is created through a series of concrete walls of variable height
5-7. Details of the floor, benches and concrete wall equipped with corrosion-resisting steel plates

Noordelijke Hogeschool Leeuwarden University Park

Completion date:
2009
Location:
Leeuwarden, the Netherlands
Designer:
OKRA, in association with Architecture Studio Hertzberger
Photographer:
Ben ter Mull
Area:
37,000m²

Project description:

For the new location of the NHL University OKRA has made, in association with Architecture Studio Hertzberger, the design for the exterior space. This consists of a solid green carpet laid out as a counterpart to the imposing building. The green grass and trees continue under the building connecting the inner and outer worlds together. A spider-like network of routes and places creates an extension of the building from inside to outside.

The large building is situated in a relatively small location as part of the park area along the river EE in Leeuwarden. The landscape aims to connect the space under the building by means of green turf that seamlessly merges to the character of the park where many cherry and birch trees can be found planted in the grass. The tree mass and the ubiquitous grass creates the experience of the garden from everywhere within the transparent building. In one corner of the building is a natural pond introduced as a stepping-stone for bats between the park and the EE.

1. The campus landscape continues the design style of the architecture.
2. River bank in geometrical shape
3. Cherry trees and birches on the lawns
4. Rest area between the lawns
5. Benches on the grassland
6. Pentagonal pond and the plastic pavement around

4

1. Front square
2. Patio
3. Terrace
4. Theater
5. Pond
6. Viewpoint
7. Expedition road
8. Concrete path
9. Community grass lawn
10. School

Site Plan

Bates Alumni Walk

Completion date:
2008
Location:
Lewiston, USA
Designer:
Ricardo Dumont, John
Hollywood, Nicole Gaenzler
Photographer:
Robert Benson

Project description:

The mission of the project as described in the master plan was to envision a new campus collaboration space for this compact urban campus of central Maine. The Bates Alumni Walk as realized illustrates the transformative power of the thoughtful integrated landscape approach in a prototypical American college campus.

The original campus had several city streets running through the campus. The existing condition for Bates Walk was one of these remnant city streets that had become a service lane with end-in parking. The goal was to convert this automobile space to a vital pedestrian district. This resultant space would serve to unite several major campus buildings along the street corridor (freshman residence, main administration, new classroom building) with a new residence hall at one end and a new dining commons at the other end.

Two iconic campus places, the Mount and the Pine Grove, exist beyond the ends of the Alumni Walk. Both of these wonderful places have handsome groves of white pine and canoe birch. The concept for the walk uses the birch as a strong informal grove to visually link these two iconic spaces. The use of the single species replicates the boldness, simplicity, and grace of the original quadrangle of sugar maples.

Bates Alumni Walk is composed to two parallel walks of 10' and 18' width (for fire egress) defining a lawn and birch grove between them. Multiple secondary walks cross the narrow space linking north and south campus districts.

Seating groupings perpendicular to the long walk are formed by parallel bars of precast seats with integrated lighting. These same precast elements are utilized in the amphitheater/outdoor campus.

The Bates Alumni Walk has connected, re-energized, and transformed the campus in the opinion of students, faculty, and board members. It has become a true crossroads of the campus where the realms of academic, civic, and social intersect.

The space has become the portal for the first year experience and the leaving graduating student.

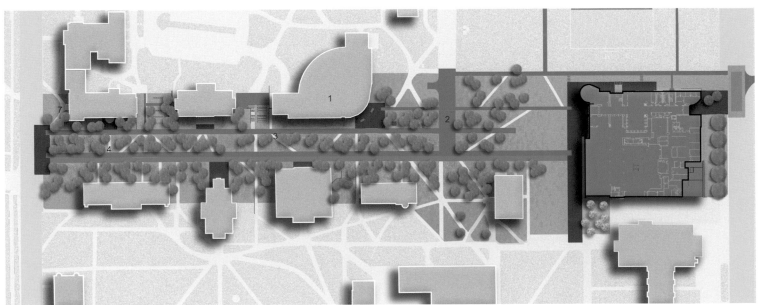

Site Plan

1. Building
2. Road
3. Planting
4. Stone pathway

1. Night view of the campus
2. The interlocking roads connect every main building
3. Lawn and groves of canoe birch along the walk
4. Terraced rest area in the lawn
5. The lawn and birch grove have become the portal for the first year experience and the leaving graduating students.
6. The simple and graceful detail design
7. Parallel bars of pre-cast seats in the rest area
8. Landscape lamps are installed under the benches.

James Square

Completion date:
2010
Location:
Quebec, Canada
Designer:
Williams Asselin Ackaoui &
Associates Inc
Photographer:
Vincent Asselin & Groupe
TREMCA Inc.
Area:
6,000m²

Project description:

James Square is a quintessential 21st century design that reinvents campus space to fit contemporary life and extends educational activities into the landscape in a sustainable manner. It highlights McGill University's commitment to improve its environment and act as a responsible institution. The project was lead by WAA in collaboration with Genivar, EGP, BPR & CS Design.

The design reflects current educational and social needs while respecting the historic heritage of McGill University's 19th century buildings. Clear, contemporary gestures complement and set the standard for sustainable practices in campus design while also reducing the presence of cars.

The project features: the transformation of vehicular streets into pedestrian alleys to increase student and staff safety; making room for pedestrians and green transportation ways; increased green space and indigenous planting; reduced light pollution by protection of dark skies; integrated artworks; handicap accessibility in a challenging sloping topography; and uprooted trees that were given a second life by a wood sculptor. Place-making transformed the square from a circulation interchange to a space where social activities and academic functions mingle in the core of downtown Montreal.

McGill's James Square redesign was catalysed by the need for major reconstruction of its underground service tunnels. Their demolition required excavation and tree removal in the central green space at the core of the Downtown Campus. The design and technical challenges of this project were enormous since the campus is built on the complex topography of Mount Royal's slopes and the buildings surrounding the

1. The plaza with modern elements combine landscaping, nature and art.
2. The steps overlooking the plaza and the retaining wall extending to the lawn
3. Feature campus steps built according to the topography
4. Terraced lawn along the stairs
5. Details of geometric steps
6. Seating area for relaxation and the gardens
7. The quadratic seats blur the boundary between stone paving and the lawn.

square were all at different levels. Parking and circulation were chaotic and dangerous and most importantly, the site had to be accessible to many users, including handicapped, throughout the construction and after.

The design goal was to create a coherent space where social and academic life could comfortably and safely extend into the outdoors. As project leaders, the landscape architects coordinated the engineer's work, ensuring the tunnel design fit under the square's levels and the emergency and ventilation shafts were properly integrated in the landscape.

James Square succeeded in many aspects particularly as a pedestrian and bicycle focused zone. Many seating and socialising opportunities were created by treating the topography as an asset rather than an obstacle and five sculptures were added to the square's cultural landscape. Increased soft-surfaces and the use of indigenous planting absorb surface run-off water and offer a refuge to wildlife.

James Square is a cultural site where landscaping, nature, art and engineering work together to provide McGill campus users a chance to fully profit from their on-campus

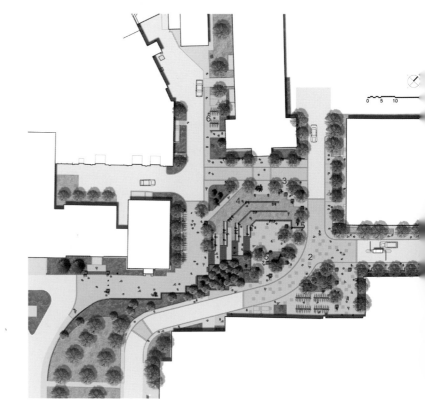

1. Milton Gate Entrance
2. Pedestrian-priority paved areas
3. Bench seating
4. Graded seating
5. Transplanted sculptures
6. Bicycle racks

Site Plan

Campbell, Salice & Conley Residence Halls

Completion date:
2010
Location:
New York, USA
Designer:
Sasaki Architects
Photographer:
Robert Benson
Area:
15,794m²

Project description:

The residence halls at Fordham are the first project implemented from Sasaki's framework plan for the campus. The buildings are situated at the main pedestrian entry to campus, near the intersection of a major city boulevard and a commuter rail line. The structures establish a celebratory gateway to the campus from the Bronx. A historic pedestrian path from the gateway is accentuated with a series of open spaces. Closest to the gateway, the terraces are a hardscape with a sidewalk café overlooking the quad. Gradually, this public zone gives way to varied paving patterns, more trees, and a more intimate green space that includes a quiet courtyard. Adjacent to several existing residence halls, the project effectively consolidates a residential neighbourhood on the west side of campus, and provides an opportunity for the area to become a mixed-use, student life hub.

The new buildings are set on raised terraces, and establish a sense of place by framing one of the most important green spaces on campus. Each of the two buildings is articulated as two towers with a shared lobby. This strategy supports smaller student neighbourhoods at each floor, reinforcing the university's focus on community. At the heart of residential floor, double-height lounges offer opportunities for socialization and group learning. At the first floor, the buildings house a café, a multipurpose room, and two integrated learning centres – key components of the halls' living & learning programmes. Even the laundry room—an often overlooked space—is designed as a social place, located adjacent to casual study areas and with direct visual connection to the exterior via a glazed arcade.

The new residence halls pick up both materials and subtle Gothic architectural patterns from existing campus buildings to create a forward-looking, mixed use village at Fordham. Brightly-coloured glazing in common areas adds a modern element to the design.

As part of the university's ongoing commitment to sustainability, the new residence halls take advantage of natural light and ventilation. Highly porous paving is incorporated into the site design and integrated with a major new storm water detention system to reduce water infiltration issues. The project has achieved LEED® Gold certification.

1. Students walking on the allée of oak trees
2. The main road and paths enclose a quiet courtyard.
3. Lawns, paths and birches
4. Lawn along the walk way

Site Plan

5. Terraced plaza in front of the building
6. The historic pedestrian path along the gateway
7. Ancient sidewalks along the main gate

Section

Ohlone Community College Newark Centre

Completion date:
2008
Location:
Newark, USA
Designer:
Perkins + Will (MBT
Architecture), Kevin Conger,
Chris Guillard, Willett Moss,
Rayna Deniord
Area:
141,640m^2
Award:
2009 Building Design +
Construction, Building Team
Awards, Gold Award

Project description:

The Ohlone Community College project is a land-use concept plan and open-space design for approximately 80 acres, including designed landscape for open space, parking, plazas, and a sustainable stormwater management system. The 35 acres of Phase 1 was completed in 2008 and established a fully-functioning stormwater management system against which development over time is framed.

Extensive research into the site's rich ecological and cultural history informed the planning and design process, resulting in large agricultural-scale approach. A series of tree windrows create a framework on the campus to create identity and spatial definition on an otherwise flat and unarticulated site.

Based on a dialogue between physical, economic, and educational considerations, synergy emerged around the estuary as a model for the educational environment and curriculum. Just as estuaries maximise energy, material, and information flows, the landscape design maximises opportunities for student gathering, exchange, and community building. Maximising social edges and creating a variety of outdoor spaces with different scales, microclimates, and relationships with the broader landscape help to achieve this aim.

1. Sidewalks
2. Building roof
3. Parking
4. Storm water garden
5. Conveyance channel
6. Detention basin/seasonal wetland
7. Wetland preserve
8. Channel to bay

Site Plan

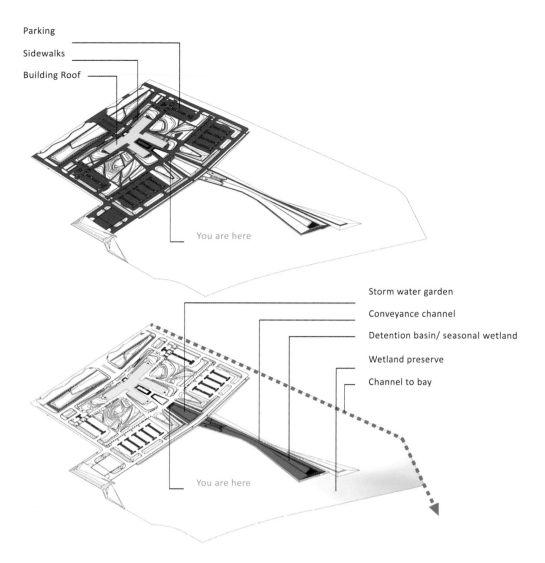

Parking

Sidewalks

Building Roof

You are here

Storm water garden

Conveyance channel

Detention basin/ seasonal wetland

Wetland preserve

Channel to bay

You are here

Evaporation

Filtration

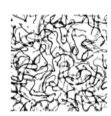

Obsorption

Microbial Action

Plant uptake

9

1. Aerial view of the campus landscape
2. The campus design includes designed landscape for open space, parking, plazas, and a sustainable stormwater management system.
3. The folded walks divide the lawn into zones with different sizes.
4. The circular lawn brings special image for the college.
5. The trees create spatial definition on an otherwise flat site.
6. Night view of the courtyard
7. Courtyard provide the students a place to rest and relax.
8. The lightings installed on the benches
9. Wood benches beside the lawn

Rissho University

Completion date:
2010
Location:
Kumagaya, Japan
Designer:
Studio on site/Hiroki
Hasegawa
Photographer:
Makoto Yoshida
Area:
344,500m^2 (incl. the campus
buildings)

Project description:

Rissho University is located in a suburban area of Kumagaya, Saitama, where the Kanto Plain and hill area meet. The pattern of urban morphology is seen in the settlements and fields scattered in the forest that supports the rich biodiversity. The campus is thus surrounded by this deep forest, enclosing a part of it within at the same time. The campus redevelopment plan therefore took advantage of this large scale and rich environment, and revitalised the campus as an 'educational institution in the forest'.

The original plan used to have a channel in the middle, dividing the school buildings and sports fields on the north and the indigenous forest, though overlooked by most students, on the south. The redefined master plan has an 'Active Zone' with new school buildings and plazas on the north, and a 'Campus Forest' with rich

greenery on the south. Those two areas face each other over a 'Water Channel' in the middle of the site. Most water is distributed from the on-campus sewage treatment facility. When looking from Active Zone, the vast forest spread beyond the water, bringing nature back to the college life. These two zones mutually complement; light/dark, active/quiet, and together they create the landscape for nature, people and architecture.

The landscape design of the Active Zone focuses on two iconic plates: Campus Green and Campus Common. Campus Green is a grand green surface stretches alongside the prefecture road. This is the main entrance to the campus, and also functions as a bus rotary area to serve the major demand for bus transportation. The other zone, Campus Common is the axis cutting through the campus. The new water channel and levee with steps boarders the plate, leading eyes to Campus Forest on the other side of the channel. To stage

the campus life of the students, the designers designed three pocket plazas on this plate: a spacious plaza facing the forest with benches to allow flexible uses, a lounge space with unique table and chairs under the existing pine trees, and an athletic field consists of basket ball courts and tennis courts.

1. The shadow of the trees projected on the graded benches by the river
2. Seats in the rest area are orderly arranged.
3. Square, waterway and trees in front of the building
4. Details of the pavement

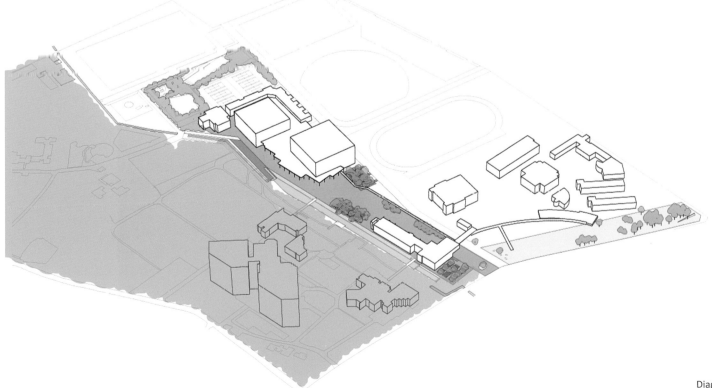

Diagram

5. Long curve tables and benches in the pocket plaza
6. Seats in front of the curve tables
7. Three pocket plazas
8. The large green space along the road is the main entrance to the campus, which also functions as a bus rotary area.

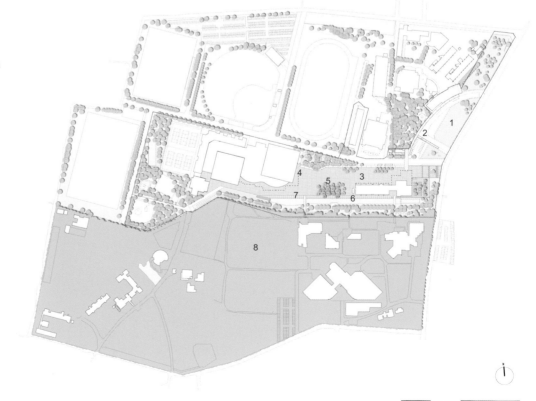

1. Campus Lawn
2. Entrance Zone
3. Campus Plaza
4. Pocket Plaza A
5. Pocket Plaza B
6. Water Channel
7. Step Border
8. Campus Forest

Site Plan

Sacred Heart University Chapel and Landscape

Completion date:
2009
Location:
Fairfield, USA
Designer:
Sasaki Associates, Inc.
Photographer:
Robert Benson Photography
Area:
12,140m²

Project description:

Working closely with Sacred Heart's leadership, Sasaki undertook a comprehensive master plan to address the social, spiritual, and physical needs of the students at the university. The plan evaluates existing facilities, establishes strategies for future needs, and elevates the quality of the 69-acre campus environment functionally and aesthetically. Upon completion of the master planning effort, Sasaki was asked to design the new chapel for the campus—the first building to be implemented from the plan. The chapel is sited at a crossroads of campus on a new main quadrangle. The chapel and quadrangle have become the heart of the campus both physically and symbolically.

Sasaki's chapel design is inspired by the metaphor of a tent, which symbolizes the long history of pilgrimage within Christian and Jewish traditions. The architectural solution emphasizes integration and diversity through the juxtaposition of both contemporary and traditional materials and forms. The copper envelope is deployed as both roof and walls, embracing both the main altar and the daily chapel. In contrast, the north wall of the main sanctuary, clad in natural limestone, is designed as a series of folds that bring natural light into the chapel, allow for vistas to and from the green, and accommodate inscriptions that inspired the design.

At the main façade, extensive use of glass emphasizes openness and transparency as a welcoming gesture to the community. The narthex accommodates ceremonies and provides overflow space from the sanctuary with a series of glass pivoting panels. Solid walnut chairs and pews outfit the main sanctuary and bring warmth to the space. The simple, white interiors of the main sanctuary provide a quiet background for the stunning mural by renowned artist Rev. Marko Ivan Rupnik.

The intimate daily chapel is accessed from the narthex and houses the tabernacle, an altar, and

seating for 40. It also contains the reconciliation room, a place of prayer and contemplation which benefits from natural light from the exterior while preserving a sense of privacy. The daily chapel's entrance is framed in glass, making it a welcoming space and providing great visibility of the Blessed Sacrament from the main entry and the narthex.

To complement the chapel, Sasaki designed a series of distinct open spaces and contemplative gardens that accommodate formal events and informal gatherings. The main outdoor plaza serves as primary chapel entry and as raised court anchored by the 80-foot-high stone campanile and bell tower. This court folds down with wide stairs to the main quadrangle, forming a podium for large exterior ceremonies and graduation. Adjacent to and serving the transparent narthex, a rectangular pea stone court features a grove of fruit trees, which provide a canopy for a series of sculptural benches and create a place of repose along a major campus intersection. On the west façade, a private court enclosed by a stone wall offers a more contemplative, cloister-like space connected to the chapel altar by a transparent wall.

1. A new quad which will serve as the centrepiece of the future campus is formed and framed by two new buildings.
2. The Chapel is embedded in a grove of native trees with rich colours.
3. Entry terrace anchored by the tower can serve as a stage for functions on the green.
4/5. The long benches installed on the walls are equipped with landscape lightings.

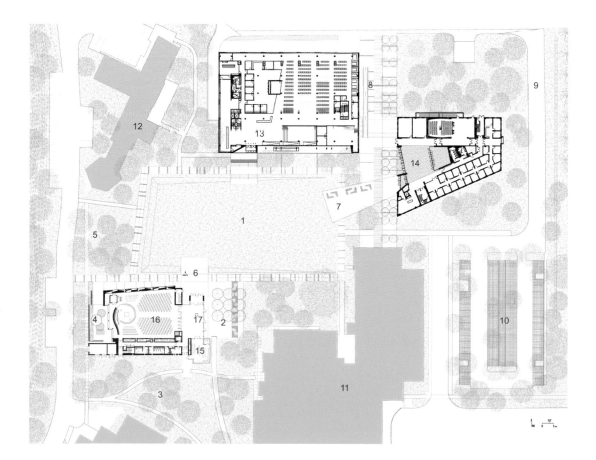

1. Great quad
2. Plaza
3. Meadow
4. Prayer garden
5. Grove
6. Bell tower
7. Forum
8. Academic spine
9. Gabion wall
10. Auto court
11. Existing academic
12. Administrative
13. Library renovation
14. Humanities building
15. Daily chapel
16. Eucharistic hall
17. Narthex

Site Plan

Seijo Gakuen University Main Gate Plaza

Completion date:
2008
Location:
Tokyo, Japan
Designer:
Studio on site, Hiroki
Hasegawa+ Chisa Toda
Photographer:
Makoto Yoshida
Area:
1,350m^2

Project description:

The plaza is located in front of the main gate of Seijo Gakuen campus. Seijo Gakuen is a private school with total education from nursery school to graduate school.

The plaza belongs to the university. However along the north boundary of the plaza, it is used by elementary school children going to school. For college daily use it is a courtyard, connecting classroom buildings and the place for students to chat. Several times a year the plaza turns in to a central area for campus festivals and ceremonies.

With this condition, the plaza needed to be a multi-functionary open space and also a place to symbolise the formality of the main gate area.

The existing pine trees are kept at the northeast corner of the plaza. By adding a couple of deciduas trees along the pine tree, lightly shaded area is made by tree foliages. In relation to shaded area, originally designed benches are laid out looking all directions. The benches have different forms and installed as a group to induce diverse conversation between students. The back of the bench is made by wood to feel a natural materiality. Also it functions as hip lest, that many students can gather around.

The plan of courtyard

4

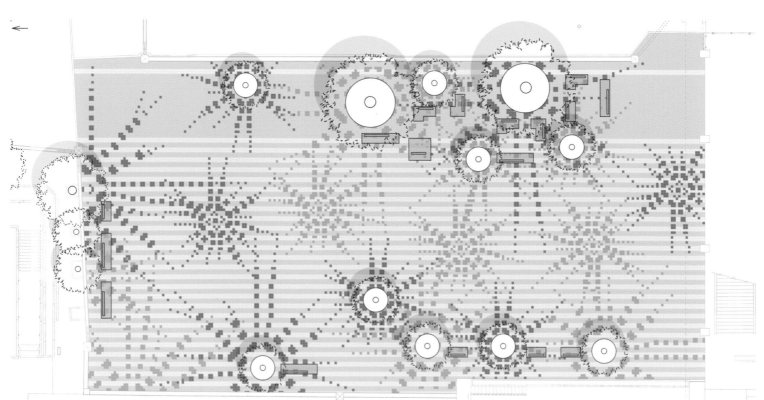

1. Looking the plaza from building
2. Existing pine tree and benches
3. The courtyard connects classroom buildings and the place for students to chat
4. The contrast between square and circular shapes makes courtyard funnier.
5. Graphical pattern made by concrete paving
6. Benches under the tree shade for rest
7. Students using benches as a group

TU Campus, Mekel Park, Delft

Completion date:
2009
Location:
Delft, the Netherlands
Designer:
Mecanoo architecten
Photographer:
Christian Richters
Area:
40,469m^2

Project description:

The Technical University of Delft gains a campus with undulating lawns and colourful trees, a campus that invites one to stroll, read, meditate, debate, eat and drink. Shaped like a bolt of lightning the promenade links the faculty buildings with one another and symbolises the interdisciplinary character of the university. The promenade is playfully criss-crossed by a grid of footpaths, reminiscent of Mikado sticks that have been scattered randomly. The formerly sharp differences in height of the park – the previous parking lots were at a lower grade – have been transformed into gentle slopes. Existing trees have been saved or moved as much as possible to form a ribbon winding through the park. Flower Fields and Prunus trees gently announce the spring. The introduction of tram line 19, connecting Leidschendam with the Technical University via Delft Central Station, establishes the campus as a car-free zone.

Mekel Park is 830 metres long and 80 metres wide. Trams and buses bring students, staff and visitors to three stops which are designed in the same formal language as the promenade. Nieuwe Delft is the name for this 832-metre long promenade, and refers to the 1,315-metre long Oude Delft canal street in the city centre of Delft. The TU Delft chose to bring the quality of the city of Delft to the campus. The Nieuwe Delft is made out of sawn granite stones and is bordered by a granite bench that spans the entire 1,547 metre length.

Mekel Park is the informal meeting place for (inter)national students and staff of the TU, and is at the same time used as a proving ground for the university. Annual proposals may be submitted in applied engineering for a permanent changing outdoor exhibition. Mekel Park is an ideal

location for university activities, such as Open Days and school Introduction Week. Future changes to the faculty buildings provide a stronger campus feel with the addition of shops, restaurants and cafes with terraces placed in faculty building entry ways along Mekel Park.

1. Lawns and forests are divided into different shapes by three crossing paths.
2. Linear paths make the campus quite interesting.
3. Tall trees in the square
4. Bridge and resting area

1. Lawn
2. Pathway
3. Basin
4. Trees

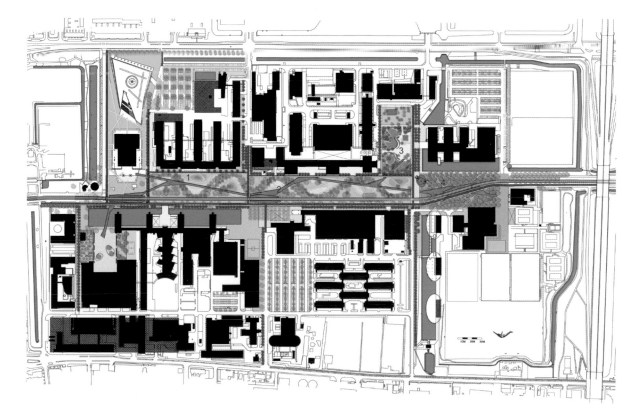

Site Plan

5. Lawn, sidewalks and bikeways
6. The existing trees on the lawns are preserved, providing a nice gathering place for the students.
7. Big stones are arranged on the paths to block the vehicles.
8. The linear paths are made of stone in different colours.
9. Joint of the paths and the main roads

University Campus Park Umeå

Completion date:
2011
Location:
Stockholm, Sweden
Designer:
Thorbjörn Andersson,
Sweco architects
Photographer:
Åke E:son Lindman
Area:
23,000m²

Project description:

Umeå University is a young university, founded in the late 1960s. Here, ca 35,000 students from all over the world study in all fields of knowledge. Umeå University is located by the coast, approximately 300 km south of the Polar Circle.

A campus park should supply with a variety of designated places with the capacity to host informal discussions and exchange of ideas. It is in the open, non-hierarchical spaces, rather than in lecture auditoriums or at laboratory microscopes that the truly creative interaction between students, researchers and teachers occurs. The quality of the campus park thus enhances the attractiveness of the university as a whole.

The new Campus Park at Umeå University consists of 23,000 sqm sun decks, jetties, open

lawns, walking trails and terraces organized around an artificial lake. The lake dominates the campus park and is located about 5 meters below the upper walkways. The shores of the lake are connected with the lower lake through green slopes, occasionally planted with shading trees. The grass slopes invite students, teachers and visitors to spend time here, studying, discussing, enjoying the view. An island in the lake is the point of departure for a small archipelago with bridges leading to the southern shore. Here, the visitor meets a hilly landscape with sunny as well as shaded vales, interspersed by the white trunks of birch trees.

In the Campus Park, promenades weave themselves forward between points of social interest. These vary in size and are sometimes larger and livelier, sometimes smaller and offering intimacy. The social spots are oriented in different directions, so that the visitor always can

find an attractive place. The promenades are of two types, one winding, gravelled path with shifting vistas and lighting in low positions, and a wider, paved promenade which connects the entry points of the surrounding buildings.

The Corso, which is the main artery of the park, connects the main restaurant Universum with the student's union. The Corso runs on a bridge over the canyon-like affluent to the lake. Here, one finds an atmosphere almost exotic right in the Northern city of Umeå, shaded and narrow, and with a dense atmosphere along a trickling brook surrounded by large leafed vegetation.

In front of the lively Student's Union, an outdoor lounge is laid out in the direction facing the sun. The lounge is a series of gravelled terraces in fan-shape, each terrace having café furnishing and shaded by multi-stemmed trees. The terraces are heavily used as a social hot spot for students and employees of the university. The new Campus Park is the result of a competition, held in 2007.

1. A beautiful lake view from the undulating lawn

2. In front of the lively Student's Union, an outdoor lounge is laid out in the direction facing the sun.

3. The lounge is a series of gravelled terraces, each terrace having café furnishing.

4. People can enjoy the lovely sunshine on the wooden terrace by the lake.

5. Stone stairs on the grassland

6. Wooden seatss on the wooden terrace by the lake

165

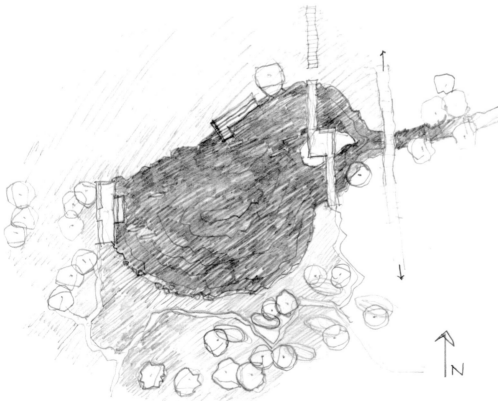

Layout of the lakeside

7. Buildings and little island in the artificial lake are connected by footbridge.
8. Lakeside view

Elevation

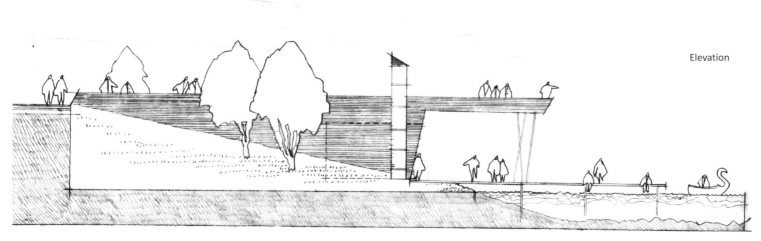

Victoria University, Footscray Park Courtyards

Completion date:
2007
Location:
Victoria, Australia
Designer:
RWA project team
Photographer:
Michael Wright and Peter Clarke

Project description:

Part of a wider development for the facilities at Victoria University's Footscray Park Campus, RWA was engaged to re-develop two of the major courtyard spaces within the campus – the Eastern and Western Courtyards.

The Eastern Courtyard (a car park) needed to shift its focus to a more student orientated space which could be used for functions associated with the adjacent Union Building, Café, Shops and The Western Courtyard has now become a unique student focused space with improved seating opportunities and places to relax or participate in small study groups.

RWA's exploratory design redefines what is possible within what are usually very staid and conservative campus landscape outcomes. The design responds to a changing campus population

by providing key elements which can be utilised in a number of different ways during different times of the year.

Both courtyards needed to function at both a campus level and a courtyard level. Access and permeability at the campus level was a key issue as there are many level changes across the Campus and universal access has been difficult to achieve. The new ramp within the Eastern Courtyard provides universal access into the space on a 24-hour basis but also provides an alternate route for all students moving between buildings.

At the courtyard level each of the spaces respond appropriately by providing enough open area to hold functions and events whilst creating different surfaces and seating forms for study, relaxation, meetings, markets and so on. The Eastern Courtyard has become the focus for

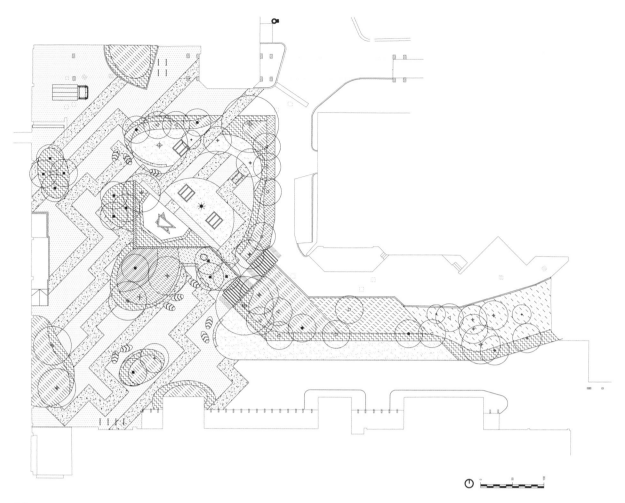

Planning map of the campus

entertainment within the Campus by providing location and power outlets for a stage and marquees where students can view events from the seating forms, tiered seating and sloped grass plane.

The new courtyards at VU suggest that landscape can become a new form of campus emblem not unlike the iconic buildings of recent Melbourne developments.

1. Both courtyards needed to function at both a campus level and a courtyard level
2. Aerial view of the pocket plaza in the courtyard
3/4. Seats, retaining wall and the ground
5. Orange seats provide a place to rest for the students
6. Seatss in geometrical shapes within the plaza
7. Grey, white and orange colours are used
8. Details of the seats

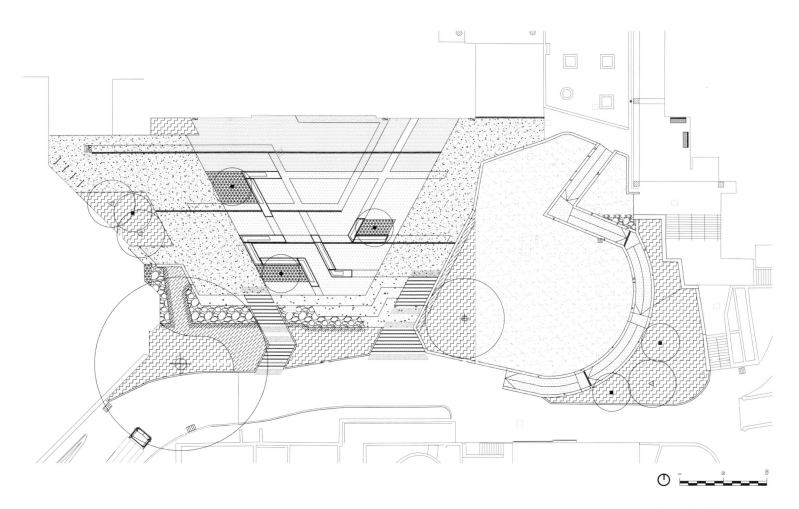

Floor plan of the plaza

7

8

Ackerman Hall in the Grove

Completion date:
2010
Location:
Monmouth, USA
Designer:
Atlas Landscape Architecture
Photographer:
Nick Wilson
Area:
9,200m²

Project description:

Opened in Fall 2010, Ackerman Hall is a 4-storey 303-bed student live-learn facility constructed in the heart of the Western Oregon University campus. The building was sited in a campus green space known as 'the Grove'. The Grove had been designed with berms around the perimeter and heavily planted with trees which were approaching 40 years old. Rather than a welcoming people space, the Grove had become a barrier and a lifeless zone in the core of the campus. By locating the building in the middle of the Grove, the architect sought to create an activity area that would create better linkages to other areas of the campus.

The building was carefully sited to retain a few select trees from the site. Other trees were milled into panelling to be used inside the building and for furniture. The U-shaped building encompasses a central courtyard that opens to the north and terminates a future residential corridor of the campus. The front of the building faces the remaining portion of the Grove which features a great lawn where graduation ceremonies and other activities take place.

The courtyard includes a storm water harvesting system as its main feature. It follows a main pedestrian thoroughfare. The arching concrete water quality channel is filled with colourful foliage and conveys stormwater to a large storm detention basin. From this system storm water is harvested and stored in an underground tank below. Water from this system is used to supplement the potable water in the building. A steel bridge connects the walkway to a plaza paved with recycled glass. The paving system is porous, allowing storm water to infiltrate into the soil. The paving system is also porous with gaps between the stones to facilitate water infiltration.

The landscape architect worked together with San Francisco artist Anna Valentina Murch to incorporate a carved granite bubbler at the head of the water channel and stainless steel spiral shapes imbedded into porous glass paving designed to evoke images of raindrops. In a driving rain the roof runoff gushes into the channel through three large scuppers. In a light rain the water bubbles gently over the carved granite art piece and drops into the storm conveyance channel.

Plants

Trees: Acer circinatum, Amelanchier alnifolia, Cercidiphyllum japonicum and etc.

Shrubs: Ceanothus thyrsiflorus 'Victoria', Cornus sericea 'baileyi', Gaultheria shallon and etc.

Grasses: Carex elata 'Bowles Golden', Carex pendula, Juncus effuses, Helictotrichon sempervirens and etc.

1. The U-shaped building encompasses a central courtyard that opens to the north.
2. The arching concrete water quality channel is filled with colourful foliage and conveys stormwater to a large storm detention basin.
3. Custom concrete pavement and plants on the roadside
4. Lawns, concrete pavement and the existing trees form a lively central courtyard.
5. Porous recycled glass paving
6. A carved granite bubbler at the head of the water channel.

1. Porous concrete pavers
2. Porous recycled glass paving
3. Porous asphalt paving
4. Storm water swale
5. Granite overflow bubbler, with storm water harvesting tank below
6. Storm water detention area
7. 'The Grove'

Site Plan

Martinsschule

Completion date:
2010
Location:
Ladenburg, Germany
Designer:
foundation 5+
landschaftsarchitekten
Photographer:
Janine Rincke, Mark
Weingart, Steven Weihe
Area:
18,000m^2

Project description:

Located on the ground of a former nursery the new school can be seen as a link between the city of Ladenburg and the Rheinaue wetlands. The main entrance of the school is directed to the city which simplifies the transportation of pupils by the school bus. Parking lots for teachers and visitors can be found at the southern border of the area not far from the entrance.

The school is developed as a diversified building of two storeys. The free space which is formed by the structure of the school building is developed into a therapeutic courtyard, a garden, a green classroom for teaching outside, a school garden to learn about flowers and plants, a workshop and a terrace which is assigned to the cafeteria. The manifold design of the entire courtyard with varying levels of heights and sorts of trees integrates the school into the existing landscape. The concept of the open space provides attractive offers to every single pupil but also to manageable sizes of groups or the whole school – from the low situated withdrawn yard to the high situated bastion with a wide view to the mountain road.

2

3

1. Main Entrance
2. Parking
3. Playground/ Sport field
4. School garden
5. Flower bed
6. Green classroom
7. Wall court
8. Landscape balcony
9. Lawn
10. Wave garden
11. Fire engine access

Site Plan

1. Parking lots for teachers and visitors
and main entrance
2. Flower bed in school garden
3. School garden
4. Fire engine access
5. Wave garden
6. Bamboo court
7. Therapeutic courtyard
8. Sit furniture

Section

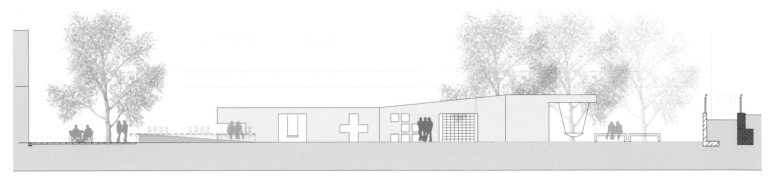

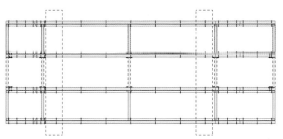

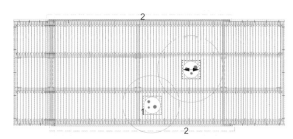

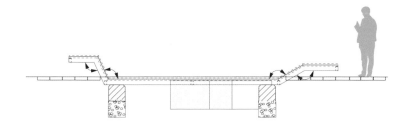

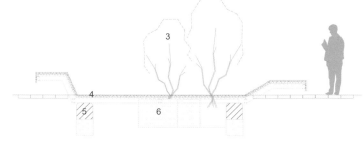

Detail

1. Wood cutout location: Stabilized frame with the same wood timber from the bottom with planking screwed
2. Slot Gutter DN 100
3. Amelanchier
4. Planking: Lark 60x29 on construction timber screws / 8mm gap Spax-screw M6x80
5. Strip foundation C25/30
6. Vegetable substrate

Oliver Hazard Perry Schoolyard

Completion date:
2010
Location:
South Boston, USA
Designer:
David Warner
Photographer:
Julio Cedano Photography©
Area:
3,035m²
Award:
BSLA Merit Award

Project description:

The Perry School site was an empty expanse of pavement with parking extending through the schoolyard, a desert programmatically and environmentally. Through a consensus-based community process with the school, neighbourhood, Boston Schoolyard Initiative and City of Boston, the landscape architect designed the Boston Harbour Island themed schoolyard and outdoor classroom richly-detailed with maritime influences. Since completion, the Perry Schoolyard has become a well-used outdoor learning and recreation resource for the school community and neighbourhood.

The Perry School is located in the dense residential City Point neighbourhood of South Boston with direct views to Dorchester Bay and the Boston Harbour Islands. In 2009, the City of Boston Public Facilities Department,

in partnership with the Boston Schoolyard Initiative (BSI), approved the Perry School's application for funding design and construction of a new schoolyard. Over the last 15 years, the BSI has developed a detailed programme for the design and function of outdoor space at Boston schools. These design standards include a demonstration woodland and urban meadow with teaching tools and lab area that enable practical application of concepts learned indoors. The programme requirements for outdoor play are established to maximise opportunities for active and imaginative play. BSI's primary goal is to 'transform schoolyards into dynamic centres for recreation, learning and community life.'

The Harbour Islands nautical theme is inspired by the school's seaside location and creates a unique sense of place with playful connection to its surroundings. The blue 'harbour' painted over existing pavement enabled this design within

the limited budget and provided the large open play/gathering space needed by the school. The elliptical track is the organising element linking play areas at the symbolic harbour islands. The outdoor classroom with maritime elements wraps around the schoolyard with buffering seashore plantings that thrive in these harsh conditions and further reinforce the design.

1. The Perry School site was an empty expanse of pavement with parking extending through the schoolyard, a desert programmatically and environmentally.
2. Students and teachers at the outdoor education space
3. Play facilities
4. Students playing
5. The fence reflects the design theme: 'harbour'.
6. Ship shape playing facilities

7. View of the gate
8. Details of the scripts on the gate
9. Scripts on the stones
10. Plants, flowers, stone pavements and stone seats

"The art of the sailor is to leave nothing to chance."
Annie Van De Wiele

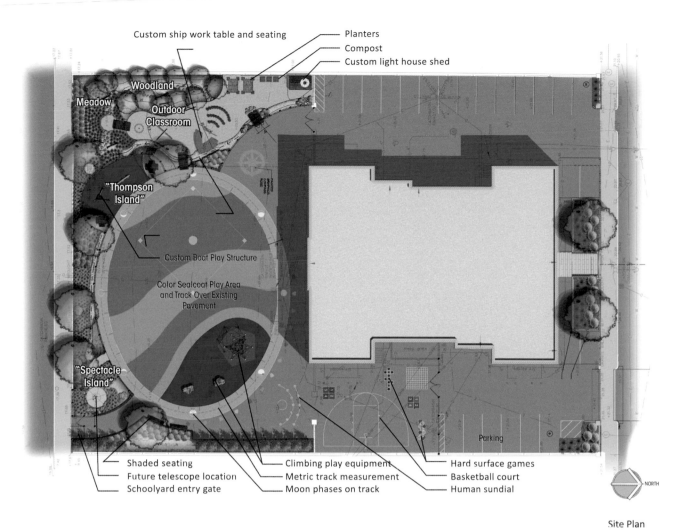

Custom ship work table and seating
Planters
Compost
Custom light house shed

Woodland
Meadow
Outdoor Classroom

"Thompson Island"

Custom Boat Play Structure

Color Sealcoat Play Area and Track Over Existing Pavement

"Spectacle Island"

Parking

Shaded seating
Future telescope location
Schoolyard entry gate

Climbing play equipment
Metric track measurement
Moon phases on track

Hard surface games
Basketball court
Human sundial

NORTH

Site Plan

Frensham School

Completion date:
2009
Location:
Mittagong, Australia
Designer:
Nicholas Bray Landscapes
Photographer:
Jules Trudeau

Project description:

Nicholas Bray Landscapes was engaged to prepare a Landscape Master Plan for the new library courtyards at Frensham School. The school is located in Mittagong 120 kilometres south of Sydney, Australia.

The project consisted of a series of terraced courtyards, pedestrian pathways, seating lawns and gardens. The objective was to unify the spaces surrounding the building and to ensure safe pedestrian access. The mature trees enclosing the garden spaces were carefully considered to maintain the old world atmosphere at the property.

Tanner Architects were engaged to design and project manage the architectural components. They were clever in developing a building that met the requirements of a leading Australian girls school. The building has large sections of glass throughout providing panoramic views of the surrounding gardens.

The northern St Francis Courtyard focuses on a central water feature. This historical core was retained with new paving and planting to adjoining garden areas. Large sandstone rectangular rocks provide seating around a circular path and allow for a subtle transition between changing heights and slopes.

Planting consisted of a mix of Australian, European, South African and Japanese plant species. The objective was to achieve year round interest, foliage throughout winter months and a rich floral display throughout spring and summer. Bold sword foliage of Dianella, Knifophia and Iris contrast to the mounded foliage of Hebe, Salvia, Rosemary, Lavender and Stachys. Silver was used generously to compliment the contemporary

building and surrounding Eucalyptus trees.

The courtyards have functioned successfully since the project was completed. The students use the spaces for active and passive recreation throughout the four seasons. It has enhanced the school grounds and brought new life to a historic school environment.

1. Courtyard, paths, lawn and garden
2. The central water feature and garden are connected by plantings.
3. Subtle transition between changing heights and slopes
4. Sculpture in the middle of the lawn
5. Seats in the courtyard
6. Central water feature is the focus of the courtyard
7. Rich plants from all over the world
8-10. Details of the plants

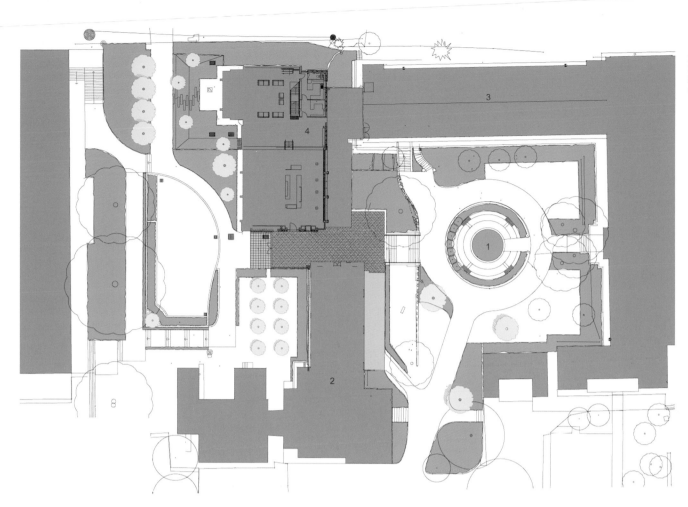

1. Pool
2. Hall
3. West wing
4. Stacks

Site Plan

Federal Boarding and High School Boerhaavegasse

Completion date:
2007
Location:
Vienna, Austria
Designer:
idealice landschaftsarchitektur
and Dipl.-Ing. Paula Polak
Photographer:
idealice landscape architects,
Paula Polak
Area:
4,550m^2

Project description:

The schoolyard at the Federal Boarding and High School Boerhaavegasse in Vienna is the first open space at a federal school developed in Austria in a participatory fashion. As a pilot project of the working group 'Open Spaces at School' at the Austrian Institute for School and Sports Facility Construction (ÖISS), it has taken on the leading role with this comprehensive schoolyard design. The yard was completed in October 2007 and had a celebratory opening.

The studio garden reflects the school's branches of training in strips of art co-designed by pupils. A workbench offers space to work in the fresh air and the opportunity to immediately present new artwork. Pupils from the ballet branch preserved footprints of the six basic ballet positions, animating others to take part. A sound element was erected and characters were chiseled into slabs.

The curved course of a stream flows by in the nature garden, occupied by native swamp and water plants. This can be crossed by steppingstones and wooden bridges. Free design and the building of weirs are still possible here as not all stones and gravel are fixed by concrete. Especially the pupils from elementary levels enjoy using this brook to jump over, bathe their feet, launch paper ships and examine the ecology of the river animals. Wooden decks made of larch with islands of plants at the side offer young people an opportunity to retreat, relax and communicate. The areas for movement are laid out with gravel. Native plant species can be found in the beds of wild shrubs, including edible berries such as strawberries, blackberries, gooseberries and aromatic plants such as lavender and curry plant.

The advanced open-air class in the stage garden makes the use of the school grounds possible for lessons. Through the implementation of

protective gravel it is also a secured jumping pit, where pupils can let off steam. The wooden deck made of larch can be used as a stage and offers a suitable framework for school events. The existing population of trees were integrated into this setting and give off shade on hot days. The sitting steps at the boarding school and nature garden are used avidly to while, run and jump. The deck is arranged with plant beds.

1. Studio garden
2. Aerial view of school landscape
3. Workbench and the colored paving
4. The existing trees are integrated into the school landscape.
5/6. Six basic ballet positions

Plants

In the garden were used natural and wild perennials, as well as
– domestic, robust pioneer species: *Hippophae rhamnoides*,
*Buddleja davidii 'Nanho Blue', Verbascum lychnitis, Dipsacus
fullonum, Daucus carota, Oenothera biennis, Plantago alpine.*
– Mediterranean herbals: *Lavandula angustifolia, Salvia
verticillata, Thymus vulgaris.*
And in the Nature Garden along the stream are: *Eupatorium
cannabinum, Lythrum salicaria, Caltha palustris, Iris
pseudacorus, Sagittaria sagittifolia, Typha angustifolia, Hippuris
vulgaris, Salix purpurea 'Nana'.*

Site Plan

9. Flower island
10. Open-air class
11. Covered class
12. Nature Garden
13. Steps
14. Gras strip
15. Terrace
16. New building

17. Old building
18. Covered workbench
19. Seating element
20. Ditch
21. Library
22. Stone boundary and water plants
23. Course of the stream
24. Wooden ramp to the wooden deck

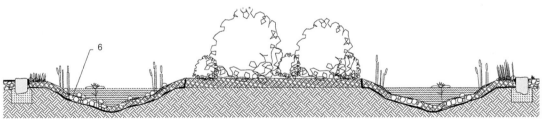

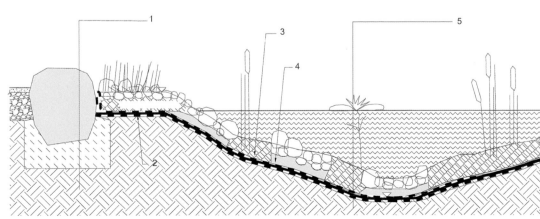

1. Kerb
   30/20/20 cm Kerb polygonal(limestone or sandstone)
   20 cm concrete foundation in-situ ground
2. Fleece under or above the foil
3. Pond substrate
4. Lean concrete about 5 cm above the fleece, foil
5. collecting basin
   10cm pond substrate or round gravel in 5cm lean concrete bed
   2mm PP protective membrane, 300g/m2
   1.2mm EDPM foil or comparable in-situ ground
6. pond substrate and gravel alternately

Section

203

7. The existing trees were integrated into this setting, and the wooden deck made of larch can be used as a stage.
8. Sitting steps and sandpit
9. Natural stream
10. Seating and native plants on the river bed
11. Steps in the nature garden and green belt use the same materials.
12. Native plants between the deck

Marin Country Day School

Completion date:
2010
Location:
Corte Madera, USA
Designer:
Willett Moss, Jamie Phillips, and Calder Gillin of CMG Landscape Architecture
Photographer:
Michael David Rose and CMG Landscape Architecture
Area:
418m²
Awards:
LEED Platinum certified by USGBC;
2010 CHPS certification (Collaborative for High Performance Schools)

Project description:

The school's campus is nestled in a valley formed by the serpentine ridges of Ring Mountain. Historically, the valley was filled with meandering streams and tidal marshes that drained the Ring Mountain watershed into the San Francisco Bay. Protecting and restoring this ecosystem, as well as providing opportunities for students to interact and learn from this habitat, has been driving the pedagogy and development of the school and its curriculum. CMG's work began with a study of broader ecological and human systems that formed the existing campus' landscape. CMG collaborated with the architects on the building massing and structure of the campus' open space, circulation, and natural system integration. A goal was to identify curriculum connections to the material fabric of the campus that included opportunities for native habitat restoration, educational hydrological relationships, and academic rituals.

The story of water's interaction with this valley encouraged the team to explore all water integration possibilities: rainwater harvesting, grey-water reuse, storm-water filtration, and native stream restoration.

The new Learning Resource Centre collects all rainwater roof runoff and stores it in a 15,000 gallon underground cistern below the Lower School Playground; the water is then reused in the building's heating/cooling system and for flushing toilets. Water metres monitor and report the amount of rainwater collected from the rooftops and used for the grey-water system – to create a comparison against the amount of potable city water usage.

All project site storm-water is filtered through a system of natural cleaning devices integrated

2

in multiple locations on the east side of campus. Upper school play area and classroom roof runoff water is directed to the upper school bio-swale and filtered through native wetland plants before being released into the nearby creek. The Lower School storm-water is directed to a bio-swale north of the Lower School Classrooms which is planted with 'fantasy play plants'— like Money Trees or Corkscrew Willows which have seed pods or interesting branches that the children can use to create crafts and make-believe games. Finally, all treated storm-water flows into the restored creek and out to the Bay.

Site Plan

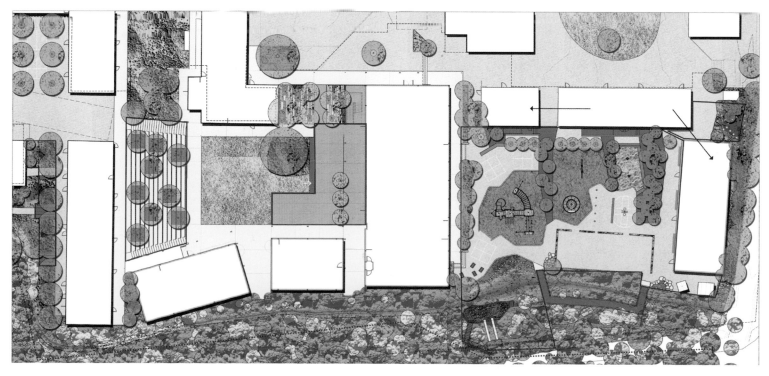

1. The school's campus is nestled in a valley.
2. Shaded benches in the courtyard
3. Wooden benches provide a space for the students to rest.
4. The landscape architects designed a honed concrete floor that passes through the pavilion.
5. Pocket plaza for lower grade students
6. Wood benches and trees on the steps
7. Recycled rainwater forms a stream.

8. A complex frame that supports
the benches is expressed in the detail
between the sustainable hardwood.
9. Benches in the rainwater garden

Ohori Junior and Senior High School

Completion date:
2011
Location:
Fukuoka-city, Japan
Designer:
Hidetoshi Furuie + Shunsuke Furuie (DESIGN NETWORK +ASSOCIATES)
Photographer:
Hidetoshi Furuie
Area:
25,380m^2

Project description:

This project is a part of the 75th anniversary celebrations of Ohori Junior and Senior High School, so new school building and play ground are built. The designers thought to create the landscape for nurturing rationality and sensitivity. In fact, they tried to create the landscape which develops intellectual curiosity and emotion of students.

Specifically, the designers thought to include the joy of finding in the landscape. So they hoped that students feel the regularity of arrangement of furniture and trees, and the order of commonality in materials and form, and natural providence. They tried to design the pavement and furniture which make students feel something significant with the years, therefore had to study the many facets of arrangement and materials etc. As a result, the expression of the landscape became simple and plain. It could say some kind of Japanese expression.

The designers hope that it will be an unforgettable landscape for students after graduation.

1. Some kind of Japanese expression
2. Hill covered by cherry trees and shrubs
3. Pond in front of the building
4. Trees under the patio
5. Semi open-air public space

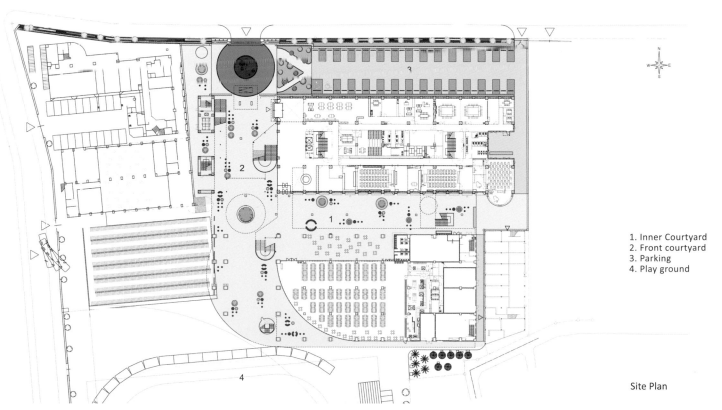

1. Inner Courtyard
2. Front courtyard
3. Parking
4. Play ground

Site Plan

Campus am Stern

Completion date:
2010
Location:
Potsdam, Germany
Designer:
Henningsen
Landschaftsarchitekten BDLA
Photographer:
Christo Libuda
and Henningsen
Landschaftsarchitekten BDLA
Area:
10,117m²

Project description:

The project takes the existing tracks and develops them to conform a network from paths, plazas and green spaces that links up all the institutions from the Campus. This area goes through a functional reorganisation where the free spaces from the school and the sport grounds are reevaluated and complemented with new public green spaces.

Two crossed bands from the basic structure: The central 'Campus Band' becomes a long straight urban open space and the 'Leisure Band' offers diverse sport and playing facilities.

Outwards is the bordering of the campus represented with walls and small fences.

That network from green areas provides versatile spaces that offers different leisure and stay possibilities as well as room for active recreational time. A part from the northern 'Leisure band' is also used by the school students.

The public spaces provide new communication places and at the same time all the paths and connections are upgraded. 'Campus am Stern' originates altogether a significant new recreational area for the surroundings.

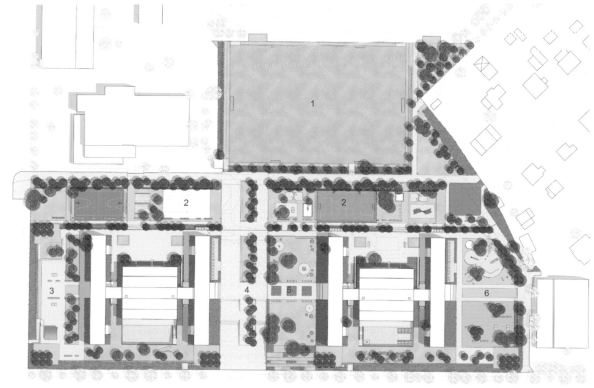

1. Sports field
2. Play, sport and Leisure time hand
3. Secondary school schoolyard
4. Campus entrée
5. Music school garden
6. Primary school schoolyard

Site Plan

1. Overview of back courtyard
2. Overview of campus
3. Overview of access
4. View of entrance
5. View of campus-park playground
6. View of campus-park paths

7. View of school plaza
8. View of children playground

School Campus in Eppingen

Completion date:
2008
Location:
Eppingen, Germany
Designer:
Dupper
Landschaftsarchitekten BDLA
Photographer:
Kristof Lange
Area:
6,000m²

Project description:

The school centre in Eppingen consists of several different types of school; a primary to secondary school, a secondary modern school and a grammar school. Each individual school area forms a heterogeneous structure of varying architecture and use of forms. Due to planned extension buildings it was decided that the individual heterogeneous building structures should all be combined according to a master plan. A comprehensive open space was accordingly developed which creatively connected each individual school to a school centre with a campus-like character. With the introduction of a (08.00-16.00), a canteen and an extension to the secondary modern school were simultaneously constructed. An entry street passed between both buildings which ran over the ground floor level of the building. This entry street was abandoned and the area extensively lowered in order to create a large central field area. Today, the school area is a vehicle-free pedestrian zone. It was possible to produce new connecting paths and visual connections through the clearance of obstacles and groves. The effect of space, orientation and safety could all be significantly improved.

It was decided that the striking oak tree which already stood there should be preserved despite lowering the level of the land. Bordered by dynamically designed walls, the oak is the central point of the campus and a favourite meeting place during break times. Aside from break times, the area offers a place for diversified festivities such as school celebrations, concerts, district festivals and flea markets.

The layout of the open space followed a uniform language and an integrated choice of material. The cost budget was limited and so cost-efficient

materials were used. However, it was possible to create a quality open space with its own special identifying character due to the underlying use of a clear form language and the creative employment of materials.

The stone blocks in the surface and walls are in varying tones of grey which form a striking contrast to the chosen colours of the foliage of the trees and the red façade of the extension. A red-leaved maple (Acer platanoides, Royal Red) was chosen as the single tree in the entrance area. The sides of the buildings are flanked by gleditsia (Gleditsia triacanthos, sunburst) which sport a fresh, light-green foliage in spring and summer and which radiate a contrasting yellow against the red façade in the autumn.

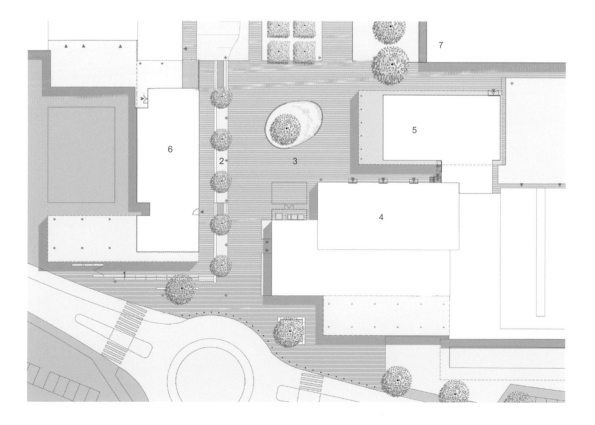

1. Bench
2. Planting
3. Courtyard
4 City hall
5. Canteen
6. Extension
7. Sport hall

Site Plan

1. The layout of the open space followed a uniform language and an integrated choice of material.
2. The sides of the buildings are flanked by gleditsia.
3. Oak trees in the courtyard have been preserved.
4. Bordered by dynamically designed walls, the oak is the central point of the campus.
5. The stone blocks in the surface are in varying tones of grey which form a striking contrast to the chosen colours of the foliage of the trees.
6. Wood benches and sidewalks

Schools Playground at Konkordienstrasse in Dresden-Pieschen

Completion date:
2011
Location:
Dresden, Germany
Designer:
evergreen
landschaftsarchitektur,
Dresden
Photographer:
Henning Seidler
Area:
2,500m^2

Project description:

The primary school at the urban district Pieschen at the City of Dresden in Saxony/ Germany is situated between a dense housing area dating back to the end of 19th century. At the schoolyard there are two school buildings which are used by different school types. Both institutions share a common green and schoolyard area. The green area is used for playing in the recreation times during the whole day.

When the design team arrived for the first time here, there wasn't so much equipment to re-use: all the about 15 year old things were broken. The available space for the children to play was much too small. In fact, there was a very nice belt of older trees around the playing area which they wanted to keep – and it wasn't easy to keep the tree's roots against the building machines during construction time. That's why the architects

just used deep-seated foundations with a small diameter or - even better – no foundations.

The team planned to expand the playing area into the complete paved schoolyard – that was the only possibility to get more space for children to play. There is a difference in height, so a small wall made of individual concrete elements was created – and by fixing some red and sunny-yellow seats on it this wall developed as a sitting wall for the children to talk to each other or for balancing over it. The sandpits were much enlarged and a wooden construction was build for a 'green outside class room'.

A Danish playground equipment manufacturer was chosen for the playground constructions – due to the children's need for movement with a lot of possibilities to climb, jump and slide on it, or to be a conqueror in one of the integrated seats. The construction is made of steel to give

maximum strength and durability.

For the children's 'Chill Area' in a small wood-like area, the design team created special sea shells made from willow wood – they are very good used especially in hot weather. To minimize the visibility from the street nearby the school wanted a screen, and the designers combined it with a segmented paintable wall in red colour with some small windows to look through and hidden boxes to keep toys for the sandpits.

For the reopening, all kids from both schools took part and occupied their playground immediately.

1. Green space and playground between two classroom buildings
2. Wood benches under the ancient trees
3. Playing facilities
4. Metal swings are more durable.
5. Children's 'Chill Area' in a small wood-like area.
6. Segmented wood fence
7. A segmented paintable wall with some small windows
8. Some red and sunny-yellow seats are installed.

Site Plan

Our Lady of the Rosary Public School

Completion date:
2010
Location:
Murcia, Spain
Designer:
Martín Lejarraga
Photographer:
David Frutos
Area:
4,652m²

Project description:

The land on which the School sits is in a new area of strategic growth in the city, in an area with public educational and cultural infrastructures: a library, high school and sports facility.

The project arises from a unique comprehensive idea for dealing with the entire block by creating a new topography to act as a reference point in this expanding zone of Torre Pacheco; a new urban, cultural and leisure area for residents, where the public space – characterised by the folding terrain and the integration of diverse uses – contains and protects the buildings.

The school is a parenthesis in the city, a parenthesis of services, education and leisure in which children face their daily visits in an attractive, safe and, above all, different manner. It is designed as a kind of jack-in-the-box, to collect

fantasies and imagination, knowledge, dreams and colour, where everything has numerous possibilities and uses: we can walk on a roof or along a wall, go to the greenhouse, to the herb garden, perhaps gym class is on the sports field today, or we are going to play basketball up on top...

The project attempts to resolve the list of requirements set forth in a simple, orderly and practical manner, integrating the building construction into the surrounding plot assigned to it, so that the architectural relationships between the buildings themselves create the courtyards and different blocks.

Thus the centre is resolved by means of several components separated on the basis of the requirements, arranged on different levels according to their uses. The pre-school building is on the lowest floor, with a separate courtyard,

and the primary school building on the ground and first floors, creating a large porch linked to the courtyard on the underground floor.

The main entrance to the school has a pick-up area, where vehicles – cars and buses – have the space needed to drop children off under the general entry porch. This plaza has an entrance and an exit, in order to avoid slowing the traffic on the streets and make it safer for the children to enter the school.

The pre-school children enter their classrooms from a ramp that slopes gently downwards, opening onto their private courtyard and connecting with the shared infrastructures zone (auditorium, cafeteria, kitchen, resting areas and general storage area).

The new topography shelters the pre-school and shared infrastructures in the most protected part, coinciding with the reference elevation (elevation +- 0.00) of the block, establishing direct relationships with the library and reading park.

The primary school children go through the lobby to their courtyard, where they line up before entering class. The central position of this courtyard makes it an outdoor activities area, which coincides with the upper floor, the roof, of the auditorium. The primary school and administration component are located at street level. The folds of the property at this level generate numerous areas of expansion for the school, which connect to the Library's Reading Park.

1. Aerial view of courtyard
2. A large porch linked to the courtyard.
3. Aerial view of school and playground
4. Main Court
5. View from the main stairs

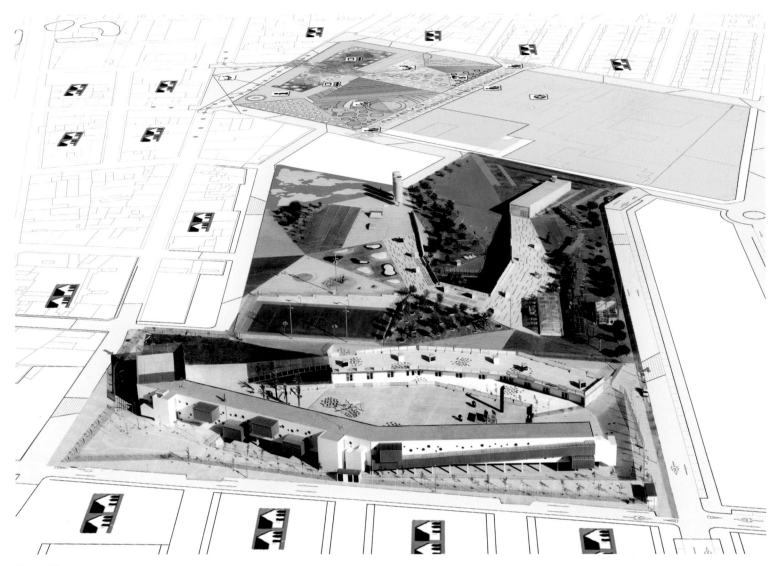

Master Planning

5

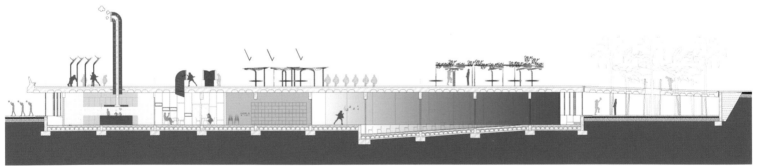

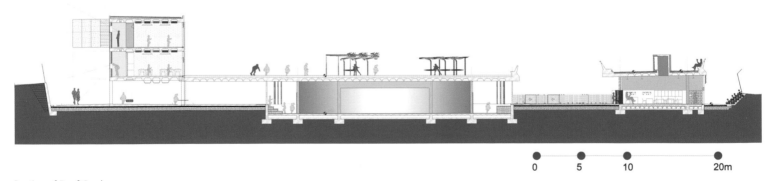

Section of Roof Garden

1. Aerial view of courtyard
2. A large porch linked to the courtyard.
3. Aerial view of school and playground
4. Main Court
5. View from the main stairs
6. Main access
7. View from the Child Court

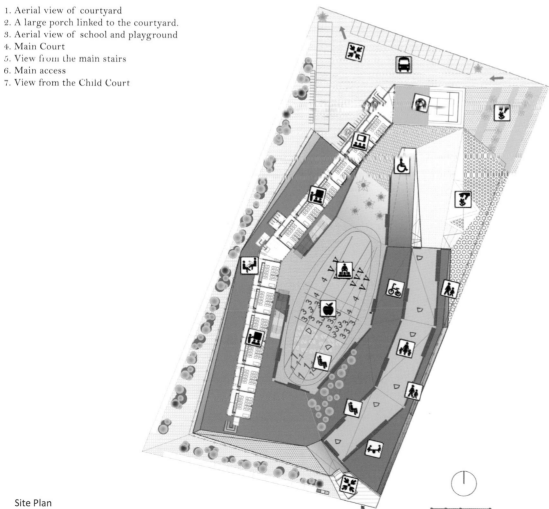

Site Plan

 Class rooms

 Garden

 Connection reading park

 Dinning room

 Special room

 Bus

 Child area

 Access

 Swings

 Conference projection room

 Sports

 Benches

243

Stamford Environmental Magnet School

Completion date:
2009
Location:
Stamford, USA
Designer:
mikyoung kim design
Photographer:
Paul Warchol
Area:
9,848m^2

Project description:

The new elementary magnet school in Connecticut features a LEED Silver design, a rain screen exterior and four prominent environmental demonstration components for educational purpose: 50% of the roofing is intensively planted and designed for active use by students; a rain garden with observation dock demonstrates the natural filtration process of rain water on site, a large holding tank below ground illustrates how stormwater run-off can be used onsite to reduce fresh water consumption for irrigation and downstream demands on water treatment systems; a wind-turbine located at the high point will demonstrate the harnessing of 'free-energy'. In addition to the environmental demonstration features the design earns LEED points for a high albedo roof for the remainder of the facility; bathrooms and locker rooms using low-flow and low-flush fixtures; ice storage to reduce energy demands during peak hours and low-e glazing along with occupancy sensors and daylight dimming to reduce energy costs and consumption.

The adaptive reuse of a brownfield site (formerly an R&D facility for Proctor and Gamble) also reduced waste in the landfills by using demolition debris as a sub-base in the onsite roads and

parking surfaces. The former Clairol Headquarters building foundation was preserved and used for the foundation of the stormwater retention centre. This rectangular form is embraced by the shape of the building allowing for rainwater to be collected on the roof and drained into a source point in this outdoor laboratory space. A series of bridges allow for students to walk through and engage directly with the evolving landscape throughout the seasons. The school integrates an agricultural area with a vermiculture farm in the overall design integrating cycles of food consumption into the educational process.

The school is designed to serve 600 students in grades K-8 and will draw students from surrounding towns.

1. School view from the roof
2. Captured storm water forms a strea.
3. Observation platform in the rain water garden
4. Integrate nature into the school design

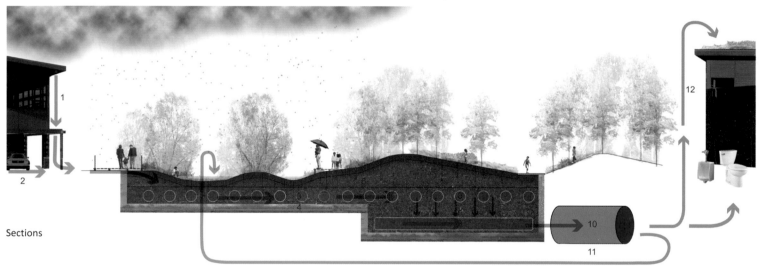

Sections

1. Roof storm water runoff
2. Parking lot storm water runoff
3. 40mm PVC basin liner
4. Repurposing building foundation, basin capacity, 375,000 gallons
5. Planting media
6. Gravel borrow
7. Storm water fluctuation storage

w/3'Φ perforated pipes
8. Filter fabric
9. 3'Φ perforated pipe for permanent storage
10. Day tank 1,000 gallons
11. Captured water re-circulated to stream inlet
12. Green roof irrigation

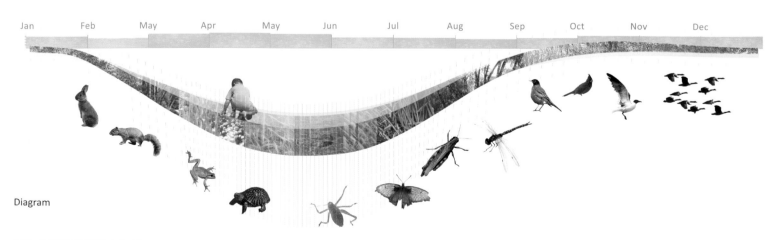

Diagram

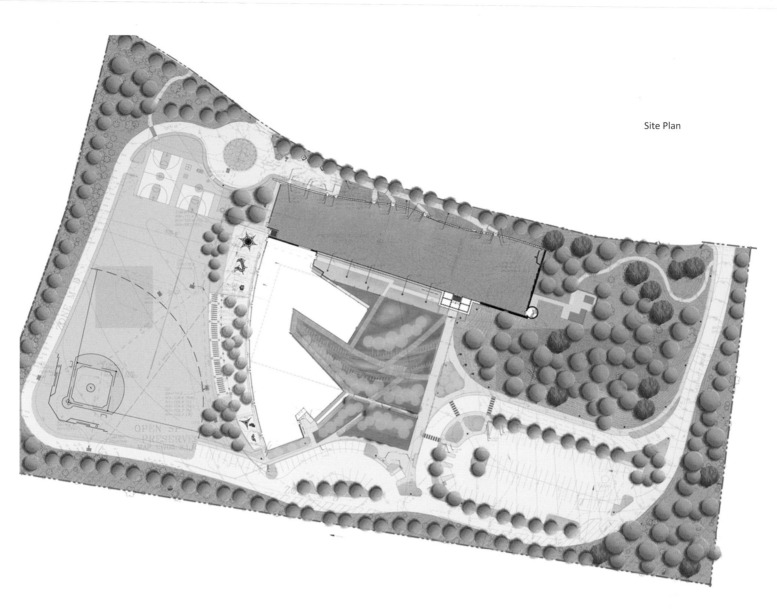

5

5. Roof garden
6. The bridges allow for students to engage with the evolving landscape throughout the seasons.
7. Bridges and the open-air experiment space below
8. Architectural structure

School Playground in Hosingen

Completion date:
2009
Location:
Hosingen, Luxembourg
Designer:
Maja Devetak
Landschaftsarchitektur
Photographer:
Wernher Böhm, Maja Devetak
Area:
4,600m²

Project description:

The new playground 'green break' is divided into two sections, one for the preschool (space structuring woody plants, small child-friendly games, hide and retreat spaces) and one for the primary (spaces for collaborative learning, as it were a green classroom, and communicative group games) .

Perfect for preschools, these groves form ideal individual hidey-holes for small children to play in. Each of the three new seating areas has its own character. The natural wooden objects are perfect for kids to climb on, and their figurative elements play to children's imaginations.

One particularly special feature is the use of indigenous tree and shrub species, arranged using different varieties to teach children about new natural shapes and colours.

The expansion of the play area for the primary school playground creates space for group learning (green classrooms) and communication-based group games (clusters of trees, go-kart, train). Imaginative natural wooden objects create an awareness of animals and encourage role-play.

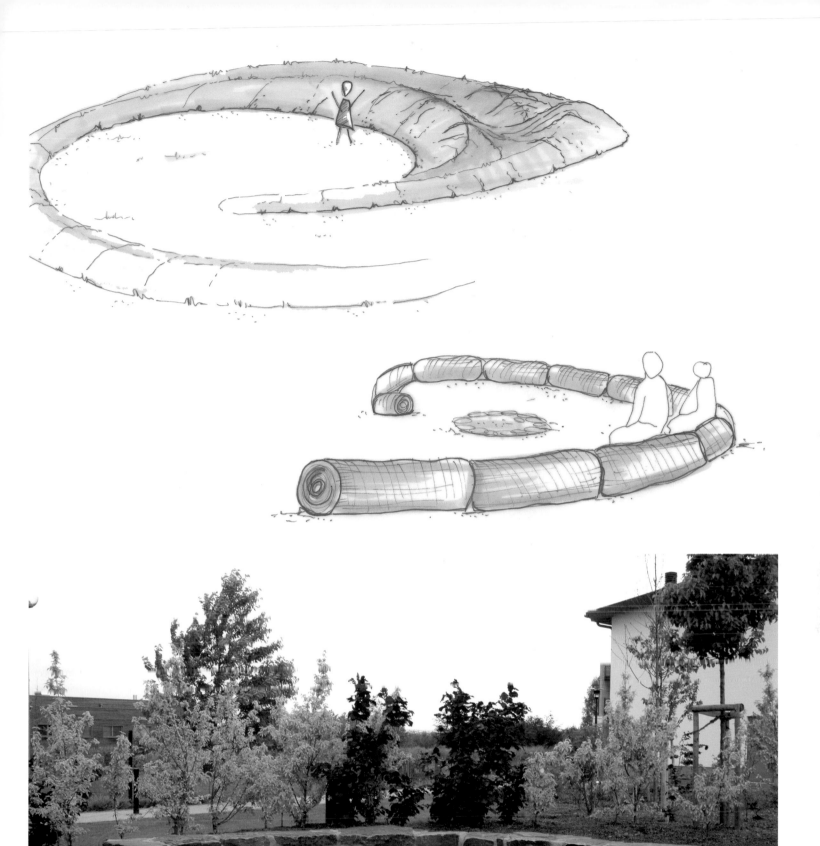

1. An intriguing winding path
2. The sloping grassland is the students' playground.
3-5. The three seating areas each have a different theme.
6/7. The facilities at the play area are made of natural wood material, suitable for climbing.

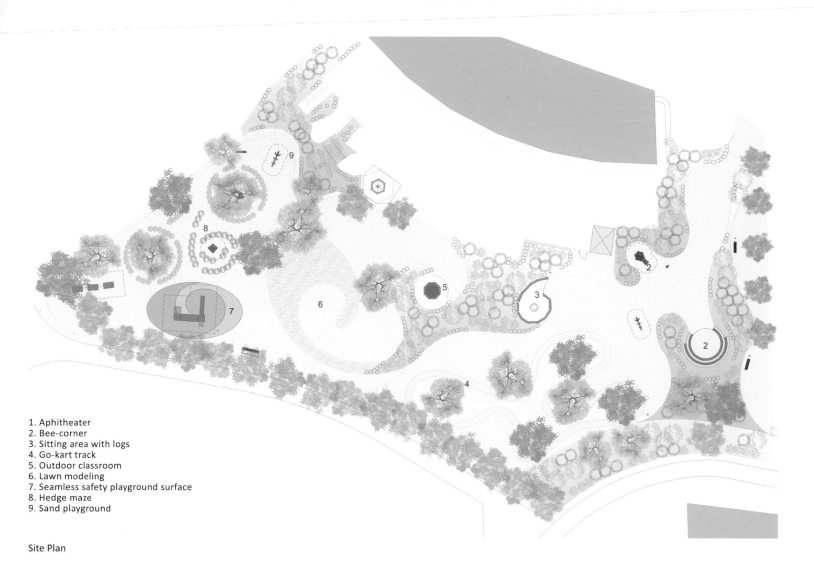

1. Aphitheater
2. Bee-corner
3. Sitting area with logs
4. Go-kart track
5. Outdoor classroom
6. Lawn modeling
7. Seamless safety playground surface
8. Hedge maze
9. Sand playground

Site Plan

8. Seating under the trees
9. Tree trunks serve as seating of great fun.
10. Details of seats
11.Details of climbing facilities

10

11

Primary School Wincrange

Completion date:
2007
Location:
Wincrange, Luxembourg
Designer:
Maja Devetak
Landschaftsarchitektur
Photographer:
Wernher Böhm
Area:
11,000m^2

Project description:

The extension of the school centre in Wincrange required a new concept of the open spaces. The leitmotiv was a diagonal opening of the schoolyard area to the landscape horizon. The landscape sight focuses through modelling of the ground, solitary trees and groves.

Other elements that underline open spaces are the lrowered amphitheatre, a lively integrated artificial lawn and large landscape stairway.

The landscape stairway connects the schoolyard lordly with the landscape in motion. The lively integrated artificial lawn in central area makes it possible to practise various sports and plays of motion. The amphitheatre descending stairs form a wind-protected space with many seating accommodations. It is possible to reach the paved ground in a variety of ways, over the stairs, climbing ramps and slides.

Elements close to nature and stimulating the movement complete the concept.

1. The vertical landscape design of the campus is very unique.
2. Seating around the tree
3. Seating on the slope
4. Vibrant wavy seats stand out in the green grassland.
5-7. The sunken amphitheatre is the most prominent open space of the project, with a lot of seating, connected to ground via the stairs, climbing ramps and slides.

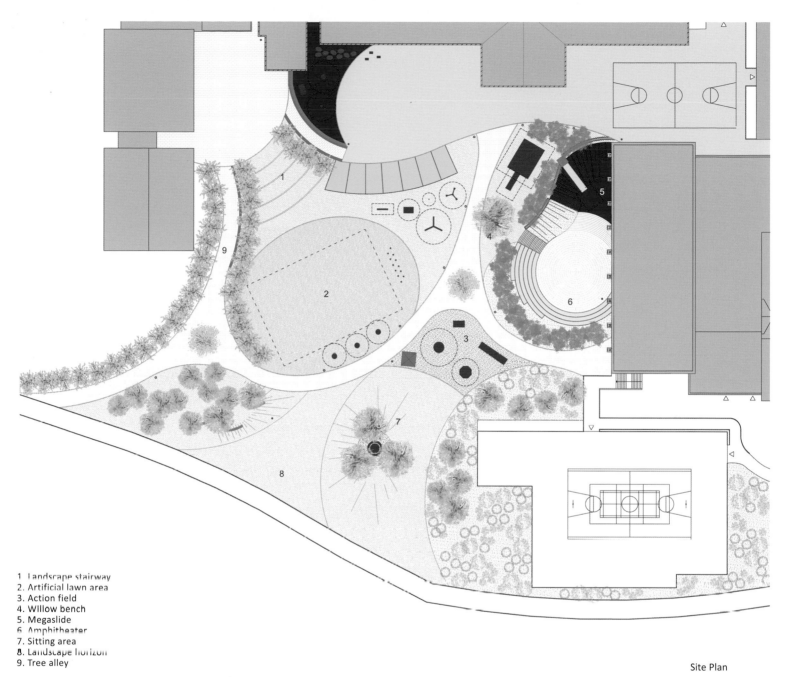

1. Landscape stairway
2. Artificial lawn area
3. Action field
4. Willow bench
5. Megaslide
6. Amphitheater
7. Sitting area
8. Landscape horizon
9. Tree alley

Site Plan

Plants

Lindigenous trees and shrubs

Materials

Local stone, wood, concrete pavement

265

Chartwell School

Completion date:
2007
Location:
Monterey, USA
Designer:
EHDD Architects (Architects),
GLS Landscape /
Architecture (Landscape)
Photographer:
Michael Rose, Patrick Argast
Area:
14,214m^2
Award:
Top Ten Green Projects Award
2009, Committee on the
Environement, The American
Institute of Architects

Project description:

The Chartwell School is a certified LEED Platinum private school for children with dyslexia. The school is located near Monterey at the decommissioned Ford Ord, once the largest military base in the United States. The Chartwell School has taken title to the oak-wooded hillside site of the Officer's Club, overlooking the Pacific Ocean. The campus is being designed to facilitate the development of the frequently exceptional capabilities of dyslexic children by providing an emphasis on the arts and the woodland environment. It has a strong sense of order and spatial orientation relative to the ocean, and a strong indoor-outdoor connection.

GLS has collaborated with the architects on the indoor/outdoor building relationships and is responsible for all site design outside the building footprint, including courtyards, circulation, fire truck and service access, playfields, and a parking lot. GLS worked closely with EHDD Architects to develop an economical site plan which uses remnants of infrastructure from the sites' former use, including roadways and grading.

The project includes landscape for Phase 1 consisting of a new gymnasium/multipurpose building and two classroom buildings with fire truck access, playfields, basketball courts, parking, site restoration with 100% coastal native plants, a nature education trail, and a system of flumes and cistern for rain water capture and reuse (designed by applicant) for physics programmes and toilet flushing. A second phase will add more classrooms and an administration building.

2

3

1. School building in the playground
2. School building in the playground
3. Night view of schoolyard
4. Rainwater collection and reuse system
5. Chair in front of the building

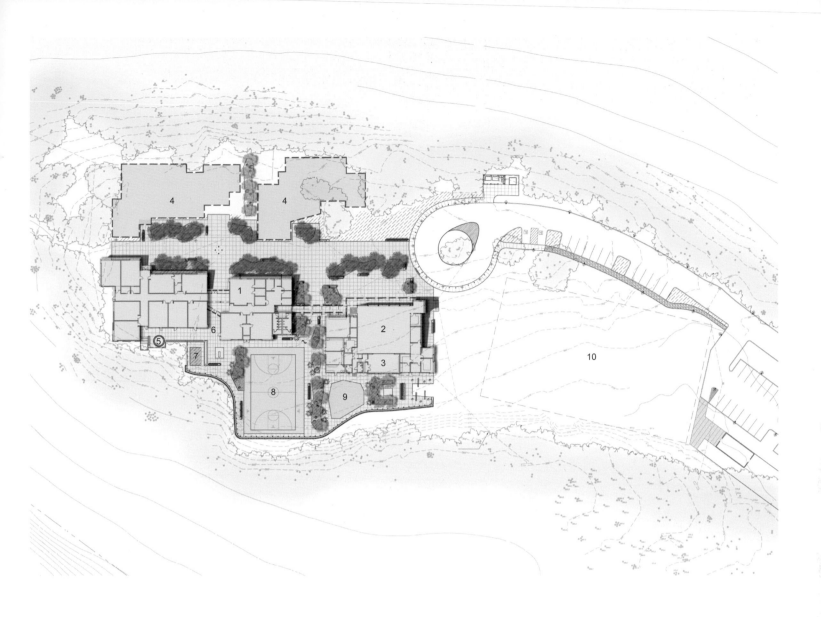

1. Classroom building
2. Multi-use building
3. Library/stage
4. Future building
5. Cistern
6. Water basin
7. Science garden
8. Basketball court
9. Playground
10. Soccer field

Site Plan

INDEX

Fax: 43 1 920 60 31 31

www.idealice.com

Network Design Associates, Inc

www.ndasacramento.com

Henningsen Landschaftsarchitekten

Tel: 49 30 69533005-0

Fax: 49 30 69533005-9

www.henningsen-berlin.de

Dupper Landschaftsarchitekten

Tel: 07136 5003

Fax: 07136 23623

www.dupper-la.de

evergreen landschaftsarchitektur

Tel: 0351-32975152

Fax: 0351-32975155

www.evergreening.de

Maja Devetak Landschaftsarchitektur

Tel: 352 90 92 52

Fax: 352 26 95 92 62

www.majadevetak.lu

mikyoung kim design

Tel: 617-782-9130

Fax: 617-782-6504

www.mikyoungkim.com

GLS Landscape

Tel: 415.285.3614

Fax:415.285.3624

www.glsarch.com

CMG LANDSCAPE ARCHITECTURE

Tel: (415) 495-3070

Fax: (415) 495-3080

www.cmgsite.com

REFERENCES

Education Development Center, Inc., Boston Schoolyard Funders Collaborative (2000). Schoolyard Learning: The Impact of School Grounds.

New Jersey School Outdoor Area Working Group (2007). Schoolyard Planning and Design in New Jersey.

Evergreen. Plants for Play and Learning.

North Carolina State Board of Education , North Carolina Department of Public Instruction (2010). The School Site Planner.

Maryland State Department of Education (2012). A Practical Guide to Planning, Constructing, and Using School Courtyards.

Planning & Building Unit, Department of Education and Skills (2010). Primary School Design Guidelines.

University Of North Texas (2002). Campus Design and Landscape Systems. Campus Master Plan.

Grand Valley State University (2008). Grand Valley State University Guidelines.

Walker Macy Landscape Architects and Planners, Thomas Hacker Architects(2007). UC Riverside Campus Design Guidelines.

1007161742

© 2013 by Design Media Publishing Limited
This edition published in Jan. 2014

Design Media Publishing Limited
20/F Manulife Tower
169 Electric Rd, North Point
Hong Kong
Tel: 00852-28672587
Fax: 00852-25050411
E-mail: suisusie@gmail.com
www.designmediahk.com

Editing: Michael Herz
Proofreading: Chen Zhang
Design/Layout: Jie Zhou

ISBN 978-988-15452-4-4

Printed in China